The Quality of Life

Also by James A. Michener

TALES OF THE SOUTH PACIFIC
THE FIRES OF SPRING
RETURN TO PARADISE
THE VOICE OF ASIA
THE BRIDGE AT TOKO-RI
SAYONARA
FLOATING WORLD
THE BRIDGE AT ANDAU
HAWAII
REPORT OF THE COUNTY CHAIRMAN
CARAVANS
THE SOURCE
IBERIA
PRESIDENTIAL LOTTERY
RASCALS IN PARADISE, in collaboration
    with A. Grove Day

The Quality of Life

by James A. Michener

J. B. LIPPINCOTT COMPANY

Philadelphia / New York

/

Second Printing

Copyright © 1970 by J. B. Lippincott Company

Printed in the United States of America
Library of Congress Catalog Card No.: 76–129673

A shorter version of *The Quality of Life* was
published in a limited edition by Girard Bank
of Philadelphia.

CONTENTS

Introduction / 7

Saving the City / 17

Adjusting to Race / 30

Education / 44

Youth / 57

Communications / 71

Preserving Our Environment / 82

The Population Cancer / 91

What We Must Do / 106

Introduction

It is appropriate in the opening year of this decade which is to witness the two hundredth birthday of our nation for us to take stock of where we are and where we are likely to go.

I am not sure that I am the man best suited to attempt this task. I have thought a good deal about our society, but I am not a philosopher. I have written a good deal of history, but I am not an historian. In the past I taught sociology, but I am not a sociologist, and although I love politics, I cannot be considered a political theorist.

But I have had one set of experiences which do partly qualify me for this task: I have worked abroad and have thus had an opportunity to see the United States from a distance, to see it whole, to see it through the eyes of others, to judge its true position in the world today. In looking at my homeland from abroad I have been struck by two contradictory facts. First, foreigners have kept me well informed on every facet of our life that is wrong. Envious critics in Europe and Asia overlook no chance to denigrate America. Newspapers eager to sell a few more copies delight in parading our weaknesses and our follies, while the intellectual leaders of all foreign nations find joy in lambasting us. Live in London, Tokyo, Rome and Madrid if you want to know everything that is wrong with the United States.

However, in spite of this constant adverse barrage, if our nation were suddenly to drop all immigration barriers, we would see from those countries which criticize us most severely an exodus of people hungry for a new life in the United States. I have never worked in any foreign nation without being approached by some of its citizens who were trying to get to America. They have told me their reasons for wanting to come.

"In your country a man has a chance to get ahead. Children get a free education. With the same amount of work you live better." And always, voiced in a dozen different ways, there is the hope: "In America I could be free." Among the intellectuals there is an added reason, which has become increasingly important: "In America you're trying to do new things. A man with ideas has laboratories to work in and superiors who will listen."

As a result of this whiplash between criticism and love I have concluded that America is a nation with many flaws which only the stupid would deny, but with hopes so vast that only the cowardly would refuse to acknowledge them. We are not much different, therefore, from

the great nations of the past: we have enormous opportunities to accomplish good, yet we contain within
ourselves the seeds of our own destruction.

I am impressed by one fact as our nation ends its first
two hundred years. We now have the oldest continuing
form of government on earth. In the last two centuries
every other nation has had to revise its form of government, most of them radically. China, oldest among the
continuing nations, has experienced change of the most
violent sort. Russia, one of the most powerful, has under-
gone total upheaval. Spain, France, Turkey . . . all the
others have tried one form of government after another,
seeking the stability which we miraculously attained.

The four nations which might seem exceptions to
this theory are Great Britain, Switzerland, Sweden and
Thailand, but upon inspection they are not. Since we
started our history as a constitutional democracy in
1789, Switzerland has been forced to change its basic
law several times, often to a radical degree. Sweden and
Thailand have shifted enormously in their attitudes toward their kings; and even stolid, stable Britain has
changed from strong kingly privileges to weak, and from
a powerful House of Lords to one which serves principally as a cautionary figurehead.

Therefore, when I look at my country, I see the oldest
continuing system of government and I take pride in the
fact that we have founded a stable system while so many
other nations did not. I think of the United States as
a rather old nation, experienced, tested, so I tend to be
preoccupied with the problems that overtake successful

and established nations. I find no sense in theories which refer to us as a young nation, for among the family of nations we are the oldest brother.

What has been the secret of our continuance? The more I think about the history of our land, the more I incline toward four explanations. They may not provide the final clue, and there may be others which men of different experience would select, but these four would have to find a place in any general analysis.

The Constitution. This is a most prescient document, a stroke of genius. It has been rigid enough to provide discipline to the undisciplined, yet flexible enough to accommodate the demands of revolutionary change. It has provided one of the cleverest frameworks so far devised, with its brilliant establishment of three somewhat competing powers—executive, legislative, judicial. Having done some work in constitutions, both here and abroad, I find it difficult to believe that two hundred years ago the men meeting in Philadelphia were able to produce such a strong and subtle plan. I think it should be accepted as a miracle, for it has never been improved upon and rarely equaled.

We are obligated to observe, preserve and conserve that Constitution, whether we are happy at any given moment with its workings or not. Events of the last two years illustrate this point rather precisely. In the autumn of 1968 the Senate, as directed by the Constitution, met to consider the wish of President Johnson to elevate Justice Abe Fortas to the chair of Chief Justice of the Supreme Court. For a set of rather tenuous reasons the

Senate rejected this nomination, which it had every legal right to do but which must have infuriated the President, who was thus denied his wish. Disclosures in the following winter proved the wisdom of the Senate's autumn decision; it had discharged one of its Constitutional obligations and in doing so had saved this nation the scandal of seeing its Chief Justice impeached. It was such situations that the framers of the Constitution had in mind when they gave the Senate the responsibility for advising the President on his appointments.

In the fall of 1969 and the winter of 1970 the same Senate reviewed two similar appointments made by President Nixon and rejected both. In these cases the reasons were not so clear-cut and compelling, and this led the President to claim that the Senate had overstepped its rights, and that if a newly elected President wanted such-and-such a man on the Court he had a right to have him. The Constitution says otherwise. It says that the President shall nominate and the Senate shall approve, and this is one of the best systems ever devised. Sometimes it irritates Democratic Presidents, at other times Republican, but I would fear for the safety of our democracy if the subtle checks thus provided were ever removed.

By conserve I mean amend. Excellent though the initial product was, it has required constant modification to keep it responsive to change, and now the time is at hand for another correction. We must improve the system whereby we elect our President, and an amendment to this effect should be proposed by Congress, approved by the states and signed by the President. I am not in favor of direct popular election, for I see much merit in the present system whereby each state controls its share of the electoral vote, but I am so fearful of electors who may vote against the mandate of the people, and of elections thrown into the House of Representatives where anything might happen, that I would accept any reasonable amendment which would remove these dangers.

Education is the second source of our strength. We were the first nation to base our hopes on the general intelligence of our population. Education has produced a people capable of choosing their own rules and governing themselves. Any changes that diminish general public education would be to our detriment.

Economic abundance has been the third factor in our success, and we should never underestimate its importance in providing us with a margin of safety when we make mistakes. One of the reasons why our democracy has tended to keep its citizens happy is that it provides them with rather more consumer goods than they would have enjoyed in other countries. The source of this abundance perplexes me. Cynics argue that we were plain lucky in having a concentration of natural resources. Conservatives claim it was capitalism, which encouraged both saving of profits and their reinvestment. Liberals point to the contributions of an educated labor force. I am satisfied that each played a role, but as I grow older and compare the United States with other nations in other cultures, I tend to base my explanation in a different area.

Religion. When I was a student, economic philosophers paid much attention to the theories of Max Weber of Germany and R. H. Tawney of England, who argued that our success stemmed from a fortunate combination in which Judeo-Christian ethic fortified capitalistic practice, forming a progressive and unbeatable team, with the success of one half contributing to the success of the other. The popularity of Marxism as an historical explanation somewhat diminished the Weber-Tawney theory, but when one looks closely at societies that operate under other religions, one comes back to the belief that Judeo-Christianity has had a towering effect upon our society and in most instances a constructive one. I think of areas like respect for contracts, the necessity of helping the less fortunate, the desirability of returning a share of one's profits to the general welfare, respect for the inherent rights of the individual. The fact that these religions have failed in such crucial areas as the prevention of war or the achievement of an equable distribution of goods must not blind us to the other fact: that they have produced a somewhat better society, in total, than certain other religions. I think America was fortunate to have developed under the spiritual guidance of these particular religions.

Fortified by these four unique supports, we have struggled along like most nations, enduring the tragedy of civil war, experiencing a great depression and surrendering many of our illusions. We have also had periods of notable vitality and accomplishment. I suppose we will continue in that alternating pattern for the next two or even three hundred years, after which we will slow down and quietly break up into new patterns, as every major nation on earth before us has done. I find this prospect no more disturbing than a typhoon in the Western Pacific; no sailor in his right mind would seek out a typhoon, but nature does produce them and the gallant seaman does his best if caught up in one. No nation would willingly repeat the paths of Greece and Rome and Spain and the British Empire, but those are the paths that nature provides for nations, and escape is probably impossible.

We are immediately concerned, however, with what the quality of American life is likely to be in the remaining years of this century. In making our educated guesses, two constants must be kept in mind. They lie at the base of everything I have to say. They limit our choice, make decisions imperative and determine to a large extent the kind of life we shall enjoy.

The first is change. Practically everything we know today will change. Points of reference will fluctuate, values will alter, capacities will be modified and opportunities will be so magnified as to terrify the cautious and delight the adventurous. It is obvious that science stands at the threshold of fantastic accomplishments, each of which will require new mental adjustments, but almost all other aspects of life also stand at the edge of change. In religion the changes in the last decade are probably greater than any made in a comparable space of time since the Reformation. Changes in morals have stupefied us and will continue to do so. Changes in the things we eat and wear and take to cure our illnesses will speed up rather than diminish. The ways we do business will alter so rapidly that those who do not grow with them will simply stop functioning, as several businesses which dominated the Philadelphia scene when I was a boy have already vanished.

Of course, amidst this accelerated change, the fundamentals of human living will continue. People will work to earn a living, they will be stormily attracted to the opposite sex, they will have ambitions and fears, and in the end they will die of the same causes that men have always died of. These permanent things are always in the mind of the novelist, but I shall not comment upon them further.

The second limiting constant is the steady increase in population. More people will crowd into our cities than did so in the past, and everything we try to do will be dominated by this one compelling fact. In the body of this book I shall mention six areas of concern—the city, race, education, youth, communications, and the environment—and in each our options will be limited by the huge numbers of people who will be involved.

Our problem is this: how can a vastly increased population, with no more living space than we had seventy years ago, find a satisfactory pattern of life in a society dominated by accelerating change?

Saving the City

History is mainly the account of what happened in the cities. There the power lay; there the wealth was controlled. The city was the center of government, the focus of intellectual and artistic leadership, and although all the food and much of the wealth was created in the country, what happened to it was determined by the cities. In rural areas there might be large monasteries, but the cardinals who dictated to them lived in the cities. Significantly, the records of history were compiled and kept in cities, so that we see history through city eyes.

Ours is the first generation in which people have had the option of rejecting the city if they wished. The automobile, new systems of marketing and communication plus the superior attractiveness of the suburbs enable us to live quite satisfactory lives while ignoring the city, but the consequences of our rejection are now becoming obvious and will color the remaining years of this century. Philadelphia is a prime example of the problems that arise when we shift from a city-centered culture to a suburb-centered culture, and the reverberations of those problems will echo along every country lane in our area.

From a purely technical sense we can dispense with the city. I was told the other day of ambitious but not preposterous plans to build a completely new executive center in New Jersey, largely underground, from which a super-community of about seventy thousand top managers would control most of the executive operations now centering in New York. With new concepts in management and new capacity to control our environment, we can run our government and our business from any preferred spot, and the city has thus lost its appeal and its leverage.

Most of the consumer services traditionally provided by the city can now be provided by the suburb. When you add the extra desirability of suburban living, with superior schools and the possibility of lower taxes, the threat to the city becomes formidable; as the surrounding areas increase in attractiveness, the appeal of the city deteriorates.

This historical change, whose ramifications we do not even yet appreciate, has come about because a series of factors happened to coincide, all unfavorable to the city. Had we been alert, we could have combatted them; we ignored them and must now work overtime to find remedies.

First, at the precise time when the automobile made the suburbs an alternative to the city, large numbers of rural workers found themselves no longer needed in agriculture, so they moved from southern farms into northern cities, bringing with them unavoidable problems in education, housing, the need for medical services, the lack of community control and the myriad dislocations that ensue when the median wage of an area has been sharply lowered, I am not distressed by the existence of these problems, for they were inevitable. Had an equal number of low-salaried city dwellers moved into rural areas, they would have produced comparable problems. What is distressing is that we have waited so long to grapple with the new conditions.

Second, with this exchange of population—for the well-to-do left as the poor came in—the tax base from which the city operates was diminished at the very time when the call for new services was increased. A family with one child left the city, to be replaced by a family with six. And as if this were not problem enough, our society began to change the rules on taxation, placing new burdens on the city. The other day a young man interested in the welfare of Philadelphia took me to one of our principal squares, stood me in the middle and asked me to look at the various handsome buildings that surrounded us. I saw some old houses of historic charm, many expensive new buildings that had been blended in with the old. The total effect was pleasing, just about what a city square ought to be. He told me, "Sixty-three percent of the buildings you see are tax exempt. In effect, they pay not a penny to the city for the services they demand of the city. And if you break down the tasks performed by the groups who occupy those tax-exempt buildings, you'll find that more than half the things they do are done for the benefit of the suburbs, not the city. This square now exists to help others, but it must be supported by us."

The same might be said of the libraries, the art museum, the colleges and so many of the institutions that have historically made up our great cities. Their advanced services are maintained principally for the benefit of others. Even the police force is supposed to see that the problems of the city do not intrude upon the surrounding suburbs.

Third, at a time when the city should have been expanding its horizons it was forced to contract them, for as the tax rolls diminished and expenses increased, we threw around the perimeter a *cordon sanitaire* of self-governing suburbs with restrictive zoning and the power to resist any attempt by the city to bring them within its political or economic boundaries. The city is thus impoverished from within and strangled from without.

There is little hope that this will change. The territorial imperative of man appears to be one of his strongest drives. Some years ago, when my political party stood a good chance of picking up some local offices because the other party had grown lax, a Congressman Green from the nearby city made the perfectly logical proposal that the lower part of our county, which was totally urban in nature, be added to the city. An explosion of major proportions rocked our county. Citizens discussed the infamous "Green Grab" from one rural hamlet to the next and allowed as how they would resist it, with their lives if necessary. My party was annihilated in the election, and I suppose a similar fate awaits anyone who proposes any kind of rational political amalgamation. The outsider, looking at a map of Texas and Oklahoma, has to conclude that the Oklahoma Panhandle ought sensibly to be turned over to Texas, but I am sure there would be open warfare if it were attempted. One could cite a dozen similar cases where nations were involved; we are probably locked into the delineations we now have, but this should not prevent us from trying to achieve workable understandings between the regional components, which may necessitate some yielding of sovereignty. Certainly, if all political agencies stumble forward for the next thirty years, each in its own blind alley, disaster of a much greater magnitude than damaged sovereignty will result.

Fourth, the freedom of any city to cope with its problems has always been inhibited by its state legislature, which throughout the United States has been dominated by rural representatives. Prior to the Supreme Court decision in *Baker vs. Carr*, which directed the states to apportion their legislatures more equitably, the cities were miserably under-represented, and many current problems began in that period. Even today, all large cities in the United States suffer at the hands of their state legislatures.

Fifth, these conditions would of themselves have

created problems, but they were aggravated by the race factor. As Negro workers from the South moved to the big cities, race was becoming a crucial force in American life. Our large northern cities were asked to make decisions for which they were ill prepared and to adjudicate conflicting claims whose roots they had not even studied. It would have been much better if we could have postponed facing up to questions of education, employment rights and public welfare for ten or fifteen years, when we might have understood those problems better, and avoided mistakes, but making decisions in such areas can never be delayed.

Finally, these historical strands came together in an age when violence was becoming a worldwide way of life. The rate of crime in our cities cannot long be endured. When more than three dozen children are murdered a year in gang killings in a city like Philadelphia, no other statistic need be quoted. The survival of the city depends upon the control of crime; without this the hopeful developments of which I now wish to speak will come to nothing, and we shall have lost one of the world's finest inventions: the complex city which has represented the best of civilization.

The city today is a kind of pressure cooker in which steam is generated with inadequate vents for its escape. Our problem is to recreate the city with new freedoms and new functions. I would propose the following:

Broadening the governmental base. It is not satisfactory to think of a city by itself. If we do, and if we constantly restrict the freedom of the city to make decisions, we will kill it, and the consequences will reach out to infect every community in the area. I cannot stress this too strongly; what happens in our cities will have its consequences in every settlement throughout the suburbs. The cost of social blight in Harlem will be paid in Westchester, and from this inevitable sequence of cause and effect there is no escape. I remember two years ago when I ran for statewide office from my peaceful rural district. Well-intentional citizens asked me hopefully, "If you're elected, will you protect us from the city?" I have often wondered if they thought we rural people could build a fence around the city so that its problems remained its problems alone. This cannot be done.

If our metropolitan areas do not find a way to govern themselves intelligently—multi-county projects, bi-state compacts—the federal government will have to take over. Therefore, anything we can logically do to speed area cooperation we must do. Perhaps a whole generation of local politicians will have to be replaced before we can accomplish what must be done, but if old ideas persist, compounding old prejudices, responsibility will be assumed by the federal government.

Let me be specific, for this is a most difficult problem. As I have indicated, I live in an attractive rural area and would not want to see it merged with the nearby city because we produce a rather more sensitive government than the city does, and we see the city wasting a good share of its tax income. But I find it preposterous when my trivial area thinks it can solve its police, sewage, watershed, educational and health problems without regard to the enormous fact that a great city impinges upon its southern border. I find it ridiculous to operate as if the Delaware River, which divides Pennsylvania and New Jersey, also divided the common problems which face any river basin. I would think that sensible men in all units of government would be studying ways to bring a sensible degree of area government into being.

Broadening the tax base. Certainly, one of our most immediate tasks is to devise ways of broadening and equitably sharing the tax base of the entire metropolitan area for the benefit of all its citizens. Considering schools alone, it is unjust that a large city with a heavy school population and a restricted tax base should be required to bear a disproportionate share of the educational burden. Relief must be found. The same is true of transportation systems and the support of those cultural institutions which serve the whole area.

Attracting power. No matter how attractive executive life in the new suburbs proves to be, I would judge that effective control will still have to be exercised from the city. Decisions will be made and supervised from the city. Therefore the new buildings that arise in the city ought to be built with executive use in mind; they should be made so attractive and so convenient that suburban alternatives would lose their appeal, considerable though that may be. Everything reasonable in way of temporary controls, tax suspension, amenities and the construction of collateral facilities should be provided, for if the power can be kept in the city, the natural appurtenances of power will stay there too.

Maintaining the marketplace. The last two decades have seen the triumph of the suburban shopping center. Perhaps the automobile makes this trend irreversible, but an effort must be made to keep the city what it has been throughout history, the major marketplace. People must be attracted to the center of the city. The stores must provide services that cannot be found elsewhere. If, in the decades ahead, it is proved that such a dream is futile and the center of the city cannot be kept vital as a shopping area, other uses must be found for it, but as of now I would not surrender the hope of keeping it alive.

Maintaining wages. There seems to be a chance that companies offering well-paying jobs, apart from executive positions, will flee the city, leaving behind only those which pay a minimum salary. This, of course, would further depress the city. Every effort must be made to keep good jobs and to attract new ones. The fact that much unskilled labor is available in the city should not be used as an excuse for making the city the center of unskilled trades. Historically the reverse has been true and should continue to be so.

Creating a transportation system. I am suspicious of most current thinking on this problem, because it seems oriented toward making things easier for even more city dwellers to switch their residences to the suburbs, which would accelerate present discrepancies. What is required is an area system which would provide three services: aid the suburban dweller who wants to commute to or shop in the city; permit the city dweller to travel from one part of the city to another; and, of greatest importance, enable the city dweller to travel into the suburbs for well-paid jobs in the new factories in the new industrial parks. Certain cities like Philadelphia, which has put together a rational transit system cutting across political lines called SEPTA (Southeastern Pennsylvania Transportation Authority), are demonstrating what can be done, but the real work lies ahead and can be accomplished only on an area basis.

Maintaining cultural services. History has usually been more impressed by the cultural services which a city can provide than by its marketing facilities; therefore, even if it is eventually proved that the markets of the central city cannot compete successfully with the convenience of the suburban shopping center, this need not necessitate the death of the city, for its major function of providing a cultural center can still be performed if some new tax structure is devised which will ensure its continuance. The greatness of a city, after its power has been concentrated, lies in its museums, its universities, its theaters, its opera, its orchestra, its baseball and football teams, its myriad other cultural and recreational facilities which no rural area can provide, and the fact that it is here that the circus comes. To diminish these is to destroy the rationale of the city. When I was a boy I came to the city and saw with astonishment its blazing theaters, its live vaudeville on the Keith Circuit, its major league baseball teams, its splendid museums and, above all, the orchestral hall to which came the musicians from Boston, New York, Philadelphia and Amsterdam. Later I came to know the libraries and the university. The city for me was an awakening so vast that I would have been cheated of one of the best parts of my life had I missed it. The other day, in comparison, I went to one of our good shopping centers and found the enticing stores immaculate but depressing and sterile. I toured the whole area and found only consumption, not a hint of creation. A child today could tour a dozen shopping centers throughout the year and not encounter one great idea such as the city gave me in abundance. Able boys and girls since the beginning of time have come to the cities for their imagination and inspiration, to witness things that were larger in concept than they could see at home. I wonder what kind of imagination we are going to develop in our children if their big excursion is to the markets of the shopping center. I remember very little of the large stores I visited as a child, but I can recall whole programs at the vaudeville theater, complete baseball games when Babe Ruth and Ty Cobb were playing, and the way pictures hung in the art museums. A city should provide growing minds with such memories.

Inviting new imaginations. In recent years I have been captivated by certain imaginative things done by cities, and I wish that all metropolitan areas had similar plans. St. Louis, in erecting that soaring arch beside the Mississippi, has created a noble work of art which lends the city a focus, comparable to the manner in which the Arc de Triomphe pulls Paris together; a city ought to have a symbol. The Astrodome in Houston was a brilliant concept, equivalent in purpose if not in architectural design to the Colosseum in Rome; both were sports palaces, and cities ought to have handsome ones. The no-traffic streets of Europe—Kalverstraat in Amsterdam and Stroget in Copenhagen—are brilliant concepts; to browse in these attractive areas, which earn their cities huge revenues, is a privilege. Perhaps such restricted streets are not practical in American cities, where the automobile plays a larger role than it does elsewhere, but a city ought to do daring and sometimes even silly things, for they excite the general imagination and produce parallel creativity in other areas least expected. The whole nation of Canada has profited from the imagination exhibited at Montreal's Expo '67; American metropolitan areas could similarly profit if they came up with creative ways of handling the two hundredth anniversary of our nation. In every city there is some new thing which waits to be done with distinction.

Re-establishing control. Everything we try will be futile window dressing if we are unable to maintain control over crime in the city. This is the major problem as we start the decade. The desuetude into which we allowed the city to fall was a natural invitation to crime and to a general breakdown of civic controls. When those who had great concern for the general welfare fled the city, those who were enemies of society were free to take over. The crime wave is our fault; it is our responsibility to end it. When a supposedly civilized city has an unbroken chain of murder, mugging and stabbing, no other index of community collapse is required, and I would place the re-establishment of control as my first priority. That it can be achieved justly and within the definitions of the Constitution I do not doubt, and I shall be referring to this matter at several later points in this book.

Reversing the population shift. Every effort should be made to lure back into the city persons who have fled. When the education of children is completed, when the heads of families grow older, and especially when life within the city is made more secure, there ought to be a return of middle-class families to the city. There is some evidence that when its older sections are rebuilt with attractive apartments, landscaped and given a community atmosphere, people who have left the city are eager to return. City living, under safe conditions, has a pulse and an excitement that rural living cannot match. It would seem likely that in the years ahead some of the most appealing residential areas in America would be found in such rehabilitated urban enclaves. This has already happened in parts of San Francisco and Philadelphia, and every city should be on the alert to identify likely areas for such treatment.

If we can take the steps suggested above, we can save the city and make it even more useful than it has been in the past. I am sure this can be accomplished, but not until we rethink one basic problem, which merits a section of its own.

Many cities throughout America are destined to have large black populations, and their surrounding areas will be influenced by the existence of this population. If the cities and their suburbs cannot learn to live with this basic fact, we are doomed. No social agency, no educational institution, no business and no political party anywhere in our country will escape the necessity of stating what it believes about race relations and then acting upon those beliefs. Delaying decisions will not mean that they can be avoided. The most remote rural settlement will be affected.

Let me digress for a moment. In the years during which I worked in Japan, a nation crushed by defeat, I frequently suspected that because Japan was a homogeneous unit, with well-defined national goals and identifications, she stood a good chance of maintaining her existence indefinitely, pretty much as she then was. I

saw that temporary defeat meant little over the long
haul, because she had remarkable sources of cohesion
and strength.

I have never felt that assurance about the United
States, for we are a volatile nation, subjected to divisive
forces in religion, national origins and race. Our very
brilliance is our enemy, our success our point of weakness. If we make a series of wrong decisions, we could
very well become a group of fragmented units while less
fortunate but more compact nations cope successfully
with lesser problems. I have said that I believe our nation will be in strong existence two and even three hundred years from now, but I base that hope upon my trust
in the American people to make certain right decisions.

Black Americans comprise 12 percent of our population. In the days of slavery our nation utilized their
skills at nearly top efficiency, and the South flourished
as our most prosperous area. Chosen Negroes, taken
from the fields, became especially skilled in the mechanical trades; they did the building, the repairing, the paint-
ing, the plastering, the bricklaying and the general care-
taking. I am not speaking as an ignorant humanist who
claims that life for the Negro was pleasing under these
circumstances; it was slavery, and we know it was hell.
I am, however, speaking as an economic biologist who
points out that in those days the human capacity of the
Negro artisan was used and that society in general bene-
fited from that use. If slavery had not ended in 1863
does anyone doubt that today the most skilled craftsmen
in the South would continue to be the Negroes? In

contemplating this, one is driven to lament the enormous wastage of human talent that has taken place since then.

For at the end of the Civil War, at the precise moment when our nation should have been casting about for radical new ways of enabling the Negro to make a maximum contribution to our society, we initiated customs which prohibited him from putting even the skills he already had to use. Negroes were prevented from doing the very jobs they had taught themselves to do best. They were excluded from the mechanical trades, were ruthlessly prevented from entering the professions and were condemned to lives of wasted talent. As a nation we adopted a policy of using one eighth of our available manpower at less than its demonstrated capacity. I know of no social or biological entity that can compete if it wastes 12 percent of its natural capacity.

I am not for Negro rights because I love the Negro but because I love all citizens. I love the grand possibilities of this nation and do not wish to see them diminished because we fail to utilize one of our greatest resources, the abilities of our twenty-five million black people.

The problem of race must be seen in this light. Whenever we cheat any segment of our population, we cheat only ourselves. Forty years ago Northerners were amused by the clever devices used in the South to keep Negroes from voting or getting an education, and so long as Negroes remained in the South the contrivances remained comic. But when large numbers began arriving in northern cities, uneducated and unprepared, Northerners awakened to the fact that now they were going to have to pay the bill for those decades of southern neglect.

The thrust of my argument, therefore, is not abstract, although abstract justice is precious to me; nor is it humane, even though I would want to be known as a humanitarian. It is practical and self-protective. I would like to see every Negro in this nation with a good education, a good job and a good salary, so that his city and state could tax him adequately for the maintenance of the services which he merits and the city requires. I want to see the Negro move up so that I can move up with him.

I have been much influenced in these matters by my experience in Hawaii, which has been somewhat ahead of the rest of the nation in grappling with the problems created by a diverse population. Much is said about Hawaii's enviable capacity to blend races—Polynesian, Caucasian, Oriental, Malaysian (through the Filipinos) —but I noticed that on Saturday nights the coefficient of homogeneity was about 98 percent. By this I mean that a Chinese social gathering tended to be 98 percent Chinese, a Caucasian party about 98 percent Caucasian and a Filipino one about 98 percent Filipino. In other words, each race tended to eat with its own members, celebrate with them and marry them. But God help the Honolulu businessman if word got out that in his store he discriminated against Orientals! School boards let it be known that Polynesian teachers had just as much chance of becoming principals as did white graduates from Stanford University. Banks promoted Chinese tellers, and the police force was integrated.

Hawaii made no attempt to pass legislation outlawing prejudice, for that abides in all of us and surfaces at embarrassing moments, but the state made a vigorous effort to outlaw discrimination and succeeded. I would not ask that our cities try to legistlate against prejudice, but it is the duty of all of us to legislate against discrimination.

An additional point must be made here. I have lived in three societies—Hawaiian, English, Portuguese—whose members lectured me about racial tolerance and asked repeatedly why America treated the Negro so poorly while they did not. I was much impressed by this until I looked around me and found that in those three societies there were no Negroes; when they did begin to arrive in England, my English hosts started behaving precisely as my homeland did. I understand also that Russia led the world in racial tolerance until Moscow began to have large numbers of African students, at which time her reactions paralleled those of England.

By and large, the United States is one of the best performers in this field. (The worst, I would say, is Japan in her treatment of the outcast Eta; next would be India.) On the other hand, we have not yet attained the equality which the noble phrases of our Declaration of Independence and our Constitution would require.

Only the occasional white citizen can comprehend the burden of injustice under which the black has had to live, and until we make the effort to understand we will not be qualified to react to what is happening around us.

For a quick glimpse into the Negro world I can think of nothing better than a reading of *Black Rage* * by two Negro psychiatrists, William H. Grier and Price M. Cobbs; it is an intelligent, nonhysterical explanation of what the black man goes through in trying to adjust to a society which says one thing and does another. *The Autobiography of Malcolm X* † is also instructive. I shall neither try to summarize the arguments made by these authors nor offer any extended analysis of my own, for this is a problem on which we must all become experts. I should, however, like to make several points.

I agree with Negro leaders that the major problem right now is twofold: get jobs and generate pride in one's race. Negroes are correct when they demand that restrictive practices which prevent them from joining labor unions be dropped. Labor unions are correct in demanding apprenticeships which ensure proficiency on the job, and responsible performance when a job is assigned. But tricky practices whereby Negroes are automatically excluded from apprenticeship are intolerable. The other day I saw a thought-provoking article which cautioned that the blue-collar worker had had just about all the pressure from would-be black union members that he would take; the author warned that if Negro pressure for union membership continued, there might be a blue-collar flare-up. But if union membership is not granted on a reasonable basis, there will be flare-ups of another kind. In fact, wherever I look today there is

* Basic Books, Inc., New York, 1968.
† Grove Press, Inc., New York, 1966.

danger of flare-ups, and the job of the intelligent citizen is not to panic when they threaten but to keep them to a minimum.

Even more important than jobs is the development of racial pride, for from this will grow all the good things we hope the Negro attains. If I were a young Negro today, I would put this first, and I say this because of a curious and heartbreaking experience I had in Philadelphia almost thirty years ago. I was sent by Washington to the large Naval Aviation Supply Depot in the northeast section of the city to see if I could help minimize certain racial disturbances which were threatening the war effort. I found the customary discriminatory practices and in trying to soften them became friends with many Negro workmen, and almost every Negro who liked me found occasion at some time or other to assure me privately that he was not really a Negro . . . or at least not an American one. Some wore fezzes and claimed to be from Morocco. Others adopted Oxford accents and said they were from Trinidad. Some even learned to play cricket and gave Jamaica as their home, and I thought how dreadful it must be to live in a society which forces a man to deny his obvious heritage. Black is beautiful, as the Bible says, and the regeneration of the Negro will start from a general acceptance of that fact.

I am therefore in favor of black studies in our schools, not because they are a well-organized body of subject matter but because they can help to create the racial pride which is essential.

I rebel automatically against the idea of having in our colleges and universities separate dormitories and classes for blacks. This seems contrary to everything we are trying to accomplish, but my reaction is so spontaneous that I suspect it may be wrong. Perhaps at this peculiar juncture in our history Negroes need separate facilities in order to find themselves, in order to determine what they must do to nail down the security to which they are entitled. I would hope that such separatism would be short-lived, perhaps only through the next eight or ten years. Indulging the demand will not be unduly costly and can be repaired when wiser counsels prevail.

If I had never lived in New England or Hawaii I suppose I would be terrified by the concept "black power," but having experienced what this phrase really means I find myself supporting it. Black power is the next logical expression of an honored tradition in American history and as such should be encouraged. In the last century, when Irish immigrants landed in Boston, they were at a sore disadvantage, for they were both alien and Catholic. They were kept in subservient positions until they learned to exercise the economic and political leverage to which their numbers and their ability entitled them. Later, when Italians arrived, they had to wrest their rights from both the old New England Protestants and the new Irish Catholics; and much later, when the French drifted down from Canada, they had to contend with Protestants, Irish and Italians. Not one of these groups was able to establish itself properly until the day when it used its economic and political leverage intelligently. In fact, the phrase "learning to be an American" could justly be translated as "learning to throw your weight around . . . within reason and within the law." I am in favor of minority groups doing so, for in this way they qualify themselves to make their contribution to American society.

This was particularly true in Hawaii. If the Chinese and Japanese had not learned to apply the leverage to which they were entitled, they would still be coolies, not because white families despised them—which they did not—but because in our system we yield nothing until there is an expressed demand. I remember when I was close to the Filipino community in Hawaii; as the latest arrivals they were at the bottom of the heap, and a low bottom it was. I told my friends constantly that their ascent would begin only when they united to elect their first official, only when they banded together to exert a proper economic leverage. Some Japanese and Caucasians, having won their own security, were unhappy over what I told the Filipinos, but I envisaged an island life which would be richer for all when Filipinos had better jobs, better educations, more political power, and more taxable income. But they could gain these ends only if they exercised Filipino power, as their predecessors had exercised Chinese power and Japanese power. Black power must be seen in this context. It will be a happy day for this nation when our blacks exert the leverage they should; we will all be better off.

One additional point is obvious. The regrettable ex-

travagances of oratory which have contaminated this
phrase ought to be eliminated; black power means historic leverage, not revolution, and I am sorry that fools
have misused this noble phrase. But up to now black
oratory has not been much worse than Irish oratory in
the 1870s. (There was a lively movement for an Irish
declaration of war against Canada with overt acts which
could have embarrassed the United States had not Great
Britain exercised tolerance.) When the inflammatory
verbiage has been washed way, we will find in black
power a desirable manifestation within the great tradition of this country.

Although I am not in sympathy with specific financial
demands made against our Christian churches by the
black militants, and although the revolutionary language
in which they are cast is repugnant, I do agree with the
leaders of some of our Christian sects when they conclude that religion has sometimes been used as an
agency for controlling the black and teasing him into an
acceptance of a basically immoral segregation, and that
it does therefore have obligations. Furthermore. I am
not much impressed with arguments that our great religions received their present endowments in trust for
the future and must not spend them now. I doubt that
a church ought to have a great deal of money; what
money it does have should be spent on the pressing problems of this day, this generation. There is an additional
problem in this area: the drift of blacks to the Muslim
religion. Islam is one of the great religions of the world
and traditionally has sought Negro members—even

though the world's principal slavers were usually Muslim. There are many reasons why American Negroes should join this church: it has an honorable history and would fit in harmoniously in the American religious pattern. But Negroes should not join Islam merely because they feel that Christianity does not want them. Christian churches should make a real effort to keep their Negro members and to enroll new ones, for it would be unfortunate if all whites were Christians and all blacks Muslim; such a dichotomy is not necessary.

Finally, twice in this book I have spoken in favor of suppressing crime. We must not use this as a euphemism for anti-black movements. It is crime we halt, not legitimate Negro aspirations. The murder rate among whites in Texas is as high as it is among blacks in Philadelphia or Detroit. When the depressed elements of our cities used to be mainly Irish, crime was also Irish, and when Italians lived crowded together in slums, it was Italian crime that perplexed us. Now Negroes occupy the unfavorable areas, and it is inevitable that they should produce the most crime. To bring this crime under control we shall have to have the cooperation of the Negro, and quarantining him in a ghetto is not the way to achieve it.

Some people who would prefer to see the Negro kept under traditional restraints take solace in the recent research studies of Dr. Arthur R. Jensen of the University of California, whose work has been interpreted as proving that the Negro suffers from inborn biological deficiencies which prevent him from equaling white performance.

The raw data from which Dr. Jensen builds his theory cannot be disputed and have long been known by those interested in the problem: in any type of test so far devised whose purpose is to evaluate either acquired learning or the ability to reason abstractly upon what might be called literary or verbal data, ten thousand Negroes always perform more poorly than ten thousand comparable whites. This has been true for Army tests, educational tests, placement tests and college achievement tests. But these facts may mean something quite different from what some adherents of Dr. Jensen say they mean. Perhaps what is being tested is not the Negro's raw mental capacity but his limited acculturation under present conditions. These may be white man's tests applied to people who have not had the white man's opportunities. Impressive as the Jensen findings appear, I would not rely upon them too heavily for two reasons: they have not yet been accepted by Dr. Jensen's own colleagues (although upon further study they may have to be), and even if they should finally be proved true, society would still be faced with the basic problem I have proposed—how to enable one eighth of our population to lead the most productive and satisfying lives.

Actually, the process of integration has gone forward rather better than I had anticipated when it started. Things have progressed more smoothly in the South than we had a right to expect, less so in the North. The riots have been no greater than I feared, and they have been of shorter duration. We are only in midstream in

this difficult process of finding new relationships between the races, and I think we are to be congratulated
that we have come so far so peacefully. But if anyone
believes the process can be stopped now, he is mistaken.

I am therefore apprehensive about any pronounce-
ment, governmental or private, which would create the
impression that our struggle to attain full freedom of
opportunity for all citizens has reached a halting point.
It has not. If the phrase "benign neglect" means a lowering of voices and a breathing space in which to assess
what has been accomplished and what must be done
next, I would obviously be in favor of it, but if it means
what I think it means, I would have to oppose it. I can
imagine no benefit that could come from halting our
efforts for equal opportunity; I can foresee grave consequences if it is attempted. It will be young white
people who will most vigorously oppose cessation now,
for they can see no justification for delay and will lead
the effort to prevent it.

In trying to decide what is just, we must not get
locked into positions which are not germane to the real
problem. For example, since I live in an area which has
been busing school children for the past forty years, and
which does so today to the benefit of all, I would naturally support busing because it has worked so well. But if
busing exacerbates those who oppose it, I would be wasting energy to insist upon something which is merely a
technique. Therefore, I would relinquish busing out of
respect for those who feel so strongly about it and who
may be aware of aspects which I have missed. But on

the matter of allowing blacks to work at any kind of employment for which they have prepared themselves I would never surrender, because for such restraint I can find no justification.

The principal avenue by which the Negro can attain economic equality is still education. Other things, like job opportunities, must be safeguarded, but the major goal remains education. The only way our cities can be revived is through education. As complexity grows, education becomes more important, not less.

Yet at the time when we must rely upon it most heavily, the system begins to show much weakness. Because we must educate everyone, and keep some in school when they have no vocation to be there, we begin to fail with many. Elementary schools have lost their power to teach reading and spelling. High schools are forced to keep in their classes young adults who are mainly illiterate and destroy discipline. Colleges suffer from revolt by their students and younger faculty members. And universities seem to have lost their way completely. All are threatened by inadequate budgets due to taxpayers' strikes or loss of alumni contributions.

Some of the heroes of our society are the men and women who strive to keep the system functioning. Some of our major enemies are those who tear it down or who, through ineptitude, force it to deteriorate. In what I am about to say it must be remembered that the large percentage of today's students get a better education than they would have got twenty years ago. It is our failure with the bottom groups that is disturbing.

I spent about half my working life in education and have always supposed that when I grew older I would return to it, for it is without question the noblest profession with which I have been associated. I have been shocked in recent years to read of schools in which teachers are assaulted in the halls or raped in the library, because when I taught I held that my first responsibility was to maintain order so that learning could take place. I did so for the students' sake; as an adult who already knew how to read and write, I could adjust to almost any kind of hurly-burly, but the learning child could not. I still believe that discipline is necessary to the learning situation. I do not mean submission or silence, for the effective learning process is apt to be lively and sometimes even obstreperous, but it must derive from evolving patterns which are kept under some kind of control.

Professional educators have quite convinced me that the basic responsibility of the school in a democracy is not reading and writing but the encouragement of children to develop those skills and attitudes which will enable them to function later on as contributing citizens.

But how those skills are to be attained without learning to read and write I do not see. Television may produce a new breed of citizen who can function adequately without knowing how to read, but even then reading will remain the master tool of civilized man. It must have priority in elementary education, and those unlucky children who are prevented from reading by psychological blocks or physical handicaps should be given remedial treatment above all else; stubborn or refractory children who refuse to learn must not be allowed to disrupt our schools. I believe in the educability of all human beings, so I would not cut the nonliterate off from a chance at education, but common sense would demand that I place him in a different kind of classroom where he would learn more and obstruct less, because the education of brilliant young people who will one day lead our society is also a responsibility of our schools.

I have been associated, one way or another, with nine different colleges, always to my betterment, but I find myself in agreement with the young people who want to improve the education which colleges offer. There ought to be more student participation in decisions. Professors ought to be more accessible to students and spend more of their time in teaching. The university should be less a training ground for entrance into the Establishment and more a proving ground for true intelligence. It is proper that the interlocking relationship between the university and the military be examined. Courses in wholly new areas ought to be offered, because for most students a well-constructed analysis of American jazz could be more meaningful than a course on medieval music.

I am strongly in favor of change throughout our colleges and universities. I still recall the shock I experienced two years ago when visiting a major university to find that the administration had placed the social and political life of the student body in the hands of fraternities which refused admission to Negroes and Jews. Fraternities have played a vital role in American collegiate education, and I see no reason why they should not retain a place on the campus if they bring their charters up to date, but to allow them to dominate campus life in the year 1970, especially if they deny membership to arbitrarily designated groups, is an anachronism, and I was not surprised when that campus exploded some months after my visit in one of the most violent student demonstrations, and one in which fraternities played a crucial role.

But even in a regrettable situation like that, campus violence cannot be condoned. It is antithetical to everything the university stands for. It creates an atmosphere of recrimination in which traditional learning cannot take place. I know that the radicals argue that during a riot learning of a different kind results—confrontation between reality and verbalized ideals—and they claim this to be the highest type of learning, but I cannot agree. The Socratic method of probing, questioning and regrouping ideas is still the sovereign path to learning, especially for those sophisticated minds who will produce the intellectual, business, political and artistic leadership in the five decades following their graduation. The commitment that results from a conclusion stubbornly hacked out of raw data is deeper and lasts longer than one attained from either oratory or emotion, and the Socratic method cannot take place in an atmosphere of violence.

Should educators call in the police to halt campus violence? Judging from the experience of Japan and Germany in the years prior to World War II, police ought to be kept off the campus. The long history of universities from Bologna, Paris and Oxford down to this day proves this point repeatedly. But recent experience in Japan and our country proves that the time can come when the police must be called in, and were I a college president, under certain circumstances I would summon them. I am not so much concerned about the protection of property as I am the protection of civilized debate. But I must stress that whenever police are summoned to a campus to put down civil protest, our entire society has suffered a grievous blow. Tradition is against it; the long experience of noble minds is opposed, and if the practice were allowed to become common, we would be on our way to losing our intellectual liberties. Therefore all connected with education ought to study ways to avoid this dreadful confrontation of police power and youthful investigation. No good can come of it. Obviously, the police are obligated to intercede when a crime has been committed, but we must not equate protest with crime.

I believe that a university has three lives: the past which accounts for its reputation, the present which discharges its responsibility to society, and the future which justifies the support and affection we extend it. The present disturbances direct themselves only to the middle responsibility, the now, contemptuously dismissing the past and ignoring the future. I would suppose that many adult readers of this book will be like me, in that much of the goodness of their lives stemmed from the experiences they had in college. To have been deprived of what Stanford had to offer, or Vassar or Notre Dame, would have been to suffer an impoverishment which would have been intolerable. A woman of sixty whose entire life has been enriched by a great learning experience has as much vested interest in what happens at Vassar today as has the beginning freshman, and an equal responsibility to see that her college moves in the right direction.

But I am even more concerned about the responsibility of the university to those generations unborn or now playing in sandboxes, especially the black generations and the children of the underprivileged, for to them the university may be their only chance of attainment. Throughout western history, and even more so in eastern nations like China and Japan, the traditional way by which men improved their society was through learning: in ancient China, learning at the desk of some sage; in Greece, learning at the feet of philosophers; in the Middle Ages, learning in the monasteries; and in recent centuries, learning at universities. No poor boy who has seen his own life expand because of education would want to see that process denied to others.

I am grateful to my college for what it gave me; I am hopeful that it can give the present generation something better; but my real concern is that in the year 2020 it be functioning so as to provide the learning without which adult life would be meaningless. I am therefore at least as concerned about what my college does today as the undergraduates who are presently enrolled. If any of them truly wish to improve their college, I am with them, for university boards made up of people over fifty are often too conservative. But if, as evidence has shown, there are among the present group of activists those whose avowed intention is "to tear down the whole structure of our society," I am obligated to respond, "Not this corner of it," and to protect it, not for its past glories nor its present good name, but because of the essential role it must play in the future.

When I first made this point in a private communication about a year ago, some of my college friends castigated me for suggesting that there could be, in the student body of my college, misguided young people who might be planning to "tear down the structure of society." They suggested that I was overly nervous or misinterpreting words, and so persuasive were their arguments that I began to waver, asking myself, "Have we perhaps overreacted to the threats of an irresponsible few who are using words in wild new ways?" Then, shortly after the publication of this book in its original form, the shocking story of "The House on Eleventh Street" in New York developed, and it was found that in the basement of this house, made available by a girl graduate from my college, young revolutionaries had been fabricating bombs for the avowed purpose of dynamiting buildings at Columbia University. What I had posed as an intellectual problem had become a tactile reality. That three of the conspirators were blown to pieces by their own bombs was a personal tragedy which we can lament, but that they should have entered into a plot to destroy a great university was a public crime which we must oppose.

Several specific thoughts preoccupy me. I am in favor of black studies if they can be kept under control. A course in black history and black accomplishment could be one of the most relevant on the campus, especially if white students take it, but a proliferating department or even a college of black studies would be slicing the material too thin and would probably be a waste of the students' time.

The history of the Negro is at least as important in the United States as many of the history courses we do teach. Certainly, we require to know more about Negro development than we require to know about medieval Spain, fascinating as the latter can be. To know about Spain is intellectual joy; to know about the Negro is a matter of national survival.

I am not much concerned about the fact that as of now we do not have a cadre of trained teachers for this subject. I was recently with the faculty of one of our greatest universities, and a young professor of history told me, "It was in July that our black students forced the administration to offer a course in black history. The president called me into his office and said, 'At this late date we can't find a Negro to teach the course. You'll teach it.' I went to a four-day crash seminar held in Chicago for others like me, spent the rest of the summer reading like crazy, and black students say it's the best course I ever taught." Education is exploring, not lecturing, and we could all profitably explore black history.

We must do something to make vocational education more attractive and acceptable than it now is. I visit technical and vocational schools whenever I can and am depressed by the paucity of students I find there. We have not done a respectable job of explaining that in our changing society an increasingly large proportion of our income will have to be allotted to services and that salaries and perquisites will rise sharply in these fields. Parents are primarily to blame, for they insist that all their children take academic courses on the chance that they might one day want to go to college, for which they will never be adapted, whereas a much better life is available through the technical school.

Looming over each of these considerations is the serious problem of how we are to finance education, especially in the city, which cannot find the taxes to pay for its schools. Radical new patterns are inescapable, and they will infuriate some of us. Public aid to parochial schools, taxation of suburbs to help pay for city education, longer work hours for teachers, a different kind of school calendar, different roles for state and federal government . . . I do not know what solutions will be found, but I know that finding them is obligatory.

In the meantime, many public school buildings under construction seem ridiculously ornate; tax dollars spent on ostentation could be used more prudently. I am distressed by any legislation which would remove the tax incentive for giving money to colleges; this is a mistake and should be defeated, for the structure of American education must be preserved, and at the upper reaches it has been traditionally supported by private gifts.

In New York state various institutions, under pressure, have consented to a system whereby young people of college age, disadvantaged in their early years, are admitted to college whether they are intellectually prepared for it or not. This seems inadvisable, because the young people thus admitted will be unable to get much from college instruction and in their frustration will insist upon lowering college standards to fit their needs. If this were done, everyone would suffer and our nation would soon lose its pre-eminence. What would make sense would be for the colleges to offer a catch-up curriculum from which successful scholars could pass directly into the regular college. If the assimilation of our disadvantaged is a pressing need, it is not unreasonable to demand of our colleges that they find ways to help such people prepare for college work; abandoning standards is not the way.

A question of exceeding difficulty will have to be

faced by our society before the end of this century. If it is proved that abandoning young children in ghetto surroundings leads inevitably to criminality, and if deprivation condemns a child to a life of lost opportunities, it seems to me inescapable that we will want to consider the possibility of establishing some kind of group home for children comparable to the kibbutz of Israel. So long as parents could keep a home together, no matter how tenuously, they would be encouraged to keep their children with them; many of our greatest citizens have grown up in such homes. But if it becomes impossible to maintain a structured home, or if parents voluntarily throw in the sponge and abandon their children, or if parents in good conscience are unable to provide a home but still want their children to have an education, such children ought to be given every chance for normal life.

Work-experience camps should be considered; many able citizens today got their start in such camps during the great depression. Such a system would benefit not only city dwellers but also those children from collapsed suburban families who merit better breaks than they now get.

Let me summarize my attitude toward American education by explaining what one suffers when he talks with European critics. They badger him with observations like this: "Everyone knows that a high-school degree from France or Germany or Israel is superior to the average college degree in America. Professor Klumper taught at Upper Oklahoma State Teachers one year and told us that most of his students barely knew how to read."

I used to argue with such critics but have lately developed a different tactic. I confess everything: "You're right, the European high school does teach more than our second-class college. You're right, we do have students who can barely read. You're right, discipline in our schools is deplorable." And I admit to all other weaknesses. Only then do I make my point: "But you must not judge your system against ours because we're trying to do something never before attempted. We're trying to educate an entire people. For every young Frenchman or German who can wangle a place in one of your colleges, we provide places for seventeen young Americans. When we try to educate so many, some are bound to be poor risks, so naturally, if you compare your best students with our worst, your system is superior. But if you put your top against our top, ours do not suffer. And we produce seventeen times as many. Our gamble is to educate everyone who looks as if he could absorb an education, and that's why our society moves ahead. That's why we draw down so many more Nobel Prizes than our population would warrant."

It is not difficult for me to defend American education, for I can tell my critics, "If I had been born in Yugoslavia or Spain, I would have had no chance for an education. From birth I would have been doomed to a limited life. But the American system was constructed so as to identify boys of promise and to make something of them."

Then I make my strongest point: "We now have about eight million young people in college. Soon it will be ten. We're the only nation in history to have more students than farmers. We have more college professors than most nations have students. And from this reservoir of trained intelligence we hope to identify those brains that will keep us alive. The loss we suffer trying to educate those who fail is insignificant when compared to the gain we make from those who succeed."

It is this aspect of American education that is worth preserving. We could educate fewer and save money, but in doing so we might miss those very boys and girls who will produce the brilliant ideas that will keep our society strong. This is the American gamble, and we must not be diverted from it.

If you took one hundred young people of almost any area, you would find that about eighty-five were living average lives, attending school with an intention of learning, preparing themselves for constructive work, and in general behaving in conformity to long-accepted standards. They form, as they have always formed, the great solid bulwark of our nation, and they can be trusted to maintain the stable services of our society. In three respects, however, this reliable majority differs sharply from similar groups we have known in the past.

First, a large percentage will experiment briefly with drugs, and of this I shall speak later.

Second, even though this standard group tends to be somewhat conservative and is not disposed toward revolution of any kind, it can become deeply agitated if it feels that wrong things are being sponsored by society, like an unfair draft, the deprivation of legal rights for Negroes, the misdirection of a university or the destruction of our environment. Then this group will listen to radical leaders; it may rise with sudden fury against an obvious injustice, creating the illusion that the revolutionary body is much larger than it is, whereas in fact the revolutionary leadership is small but has been clever enough to capitalize on a conspicuous weakness. The great body of youth remains basically conservative.

The third characteristic of this majority is one which has gained the most notoriety and which is most difficult for parents to understand or accept. Unquestionably a new and more relaxed morality guides the young. The evidence is too overwhelming to be ignored; when one of our finest colleges permits men students to entertain women in dormitory rooms providing only that the girls leave by four in the morning, a change of such dramatic quality has occurred that people of my generation can barely comprehend it. Even so, the changes so far as I can judge now seem to be for the better. Certainly, they have not corrupted youth or destroyed the family, as some predicted they would. Boys and girls today seem to handle sex somewhat more effectively than we did fifty years ago, but the great permanent problems remain as they were and have been little affected by the new morality. Young men still want a home and will pay a great price to get one; most women still feel more secure if they have husbands to father and care for their children; families are still the most logical way to raise children; the permanent problem of sex is not how to handle the fires of adolescence or the first chaotic and delightful years of marriage and early parenthood but how to live creatively with a partner from the age of thirty-five to seventy—the new morality has had little effect upon these basic problems. The only significant change I have seen is that careless schoolgirls tend to become pregnant at an earlier age, and this is regrettable, but I doubt that the percentage of girls who are pregnant when they marry has altered from what it was fifty years ago.

We now come to a major change. If the average youth today tends to be pretty much as he always was, the highly gifted youth tends to be more mercurial. If I say the 85 percent of the young people today resemble young people of all former periods, this means that 15 percent have changed, and with shocking frequency they tend to be the most able ones. The radical leadership of the young comes most often from the most brilliant. In the decades ahead it will be these young leaders, sobered by responsibility, who will give this nation much of its direction, and this is necessary for the development of a strong society. Nothing could be more damaging than for us to reject the young radical leaders because, for the time being, we find their aspirations unpalatable. They are noisy, unkempt, often ill mannered, but they point to the problems that will occupy us for the decades ahead, and it would be folly to dismiss the aid they can give us.

It should be obvious that in the preceding paragraph I am differentiating between the historic radical who wants to change society by the use of accepted if noisy

means and the new type of revolutionary who boasts
that he wishes to tear down the whole structure. We
must listen to the first and oppose the second; we must
adjust our thinking to what the first says and keep the
latter under control, using police power and the courts
if necessary.

I see the future as a combination of the constructive
work of the stable 85 percent joined with the proliferating ideas of the radical leadership. I suppose that is
about the right mix for a democracy, and if one looks
for a single reason why the United States has flourished
in contrast with certain other nations, it must be because
we have had this fruitful amalgam of continuing work
plus advanced thinking. Anyone who believes that the
former alone can secure national well-being is ill advised.

I am very hopeful about our young people. As I see
them in a variety of situations, and in many foreign
countries, I find them somewhat better educated than I
was at their age, taller, keener, more committed to
achieving a good life. They can't spell as well as I did
nor do they know as much history; most of them have
not worked as much as I did, but they have traveled
more and they have larger vocabularies. When I try to
form an opinion about today's young people, I keep two
facts in mind: I used to play a lot of basketball and was
on two championship teams, but no one I played with
or against could even make one of the good teams today.
Also, in the period from 1934 through 1939 I heard a
good deal about the degeneration of our youth, their
flabbiness, their lack of concern, but two years later I

watched as these same young men fought at Guadal-
canal and the other hell holes of the Pacific, and they
were somewhat better able to adjust to those dreadful
conditions than were the Japanese. I would suspect that
if this nation were again seriously threatened, the same
situation would prevail.

It is more difficult to be a young person today than it
was fifty years ago. What could happen to a young
person in 1920? He could steal and find himself with a
court record; or he could become a drunk; or he could
contract a venereal disease, and that was about it. Today
the young person is confronted by four new problems
(or old problems made more difficult) and each is more
destructive than what the 1920 young person had to face:
the draft, drugs, the new public acceptance of homosexuality and, worst of all, a general disaffection with life,
an alienation from our society.

1. The draft, as it operated through November, 1969,
was a monstrous affront to our young people, men and
women alike, for it was used to support an unpopular
war and of itself generated deceit, alienation and profound moral confusion. It was a system that boys from
well-to-do families could escape and boys who did well
in college could evade; other boys, who had no vocation
for teaching, could find shameful refuge in elementary-
school classrooms in which they did much damage. I was
moved by the number of young people I met who were
morally repelled by the system which they themselves
profited from, and many, after accepting two or three
years of such refuge, found that they had to submit

themselves to the draft, as an act of human decency. The new system of lottery by birthday is a significant improvement.

2. It is difficult these days to say anything sensible when writing about drugs. After considerable work in this field I have reached certain conclusions which will affect my readers in one of three ways: people my age with no children will judge me irresponsible; couples with children will read attentively and with some sense of recognition, for they live with this problem; and I hope that those under twenty-five will say, "At least he's thought about it." In the meantime, all of us take refuge in old laws that may or may not be the ones we will want when we know more.

I have never met anyone who took heroin for any extended period whose life was not ruined. There may be people who have succeeded in breaking the habit and have returned to normal lives, but I don't know them. The penalty that heroin exacts from its users is so devastating that anyone who carelessly stumbles into its trap is condemning himself to misery; anyone who knowingly entraps another, or who sells heroin for a profit, ought to be jailed for life. I would rather lose my left arm than risk the terrors of heroin.

LSD appears to be too dangerous to use without medical supervision. It has produced disastrous results in some individuals, so that though the testimony is strong that it can produce exhilarating results in those able to control it, the risk involved is probably so great that one would be well advised to avoid it. I would suppose that when the data are all in, LSD will be found to be a highly dangerous drug with certain carefully defined therapeutic uses if administered in clinical surroundings. Its general use will pretty surely be restricted, and the casual user who tries it on his own will do so at considerable risk. I would not touch LSD, principally because I would be afraid of its consequences but also because my mind is already so expanded with ideas, music, speculation and the joy of nature that if it were expanded further by drugs it would probably burst. I am all for expanding the minds of young people, but this can best be done with ideas and the capacity to witness the infinite richness of natural things.

Marijuana raises problems which are especially perplexing in that even though the drug is an ancient one, with many nations having used it extensively through the past two thousand years, we know little about it. Many Americans have experimented with it, and while final results are not yet in, these facts appear to be true: most casual users are able to back away from marijuana without suffering lasting effects, and the criminal penalties for its possession seem excessive.

Two nagging questions persist. Does marijuana lead to escalation to more dangerous drugs, and does it induce a general lassitude which destroys will? Testimony is apparently strong that marijuana of itself is not addictive and therefore does not lead to an automatic physiological escalation, but I can affirm that the social milieu in which it is smoked does tempt one to further experimentation, often of a most disastrous sort. What

I am saying is this: marijuana doesn't lead to heroin, but the gang with whom you smoke it may. Marijuana is not addictive; but the social atmosphere that surrounds it is; thus it can be argued, "Marijuana does lead to heroin," but not in the sense usually implied.

Judging from the performance of those nations which have long used marijuana, it does induce a lethargy which encourages its users to "drop out" and must therefore be considered as antithetical to the interests of society. There is mounting evidence that extended use will produce the same effect in the United States.

I am not much impressed with the argument that marijuana is to the young what a martini or a cigarette is to the adult; there is a substantial difference in that the milieu of cigarette smoking does not lead to heroin, nor does a cocktail lead to the social indifference which penalizes the marijuana countries. As for the argument that taking opium did not prevent Thomas DeQuincey from writing well, I have never been overly excited by his results.

It would not be illogical to outlaw marijuana while condoning alcohol. What is illogical is the ultra-severe legal penalty for the possession of one and not the other. If the severe laws against possession of marijuana are kept on the books, and if millions of people continue to smoke it, obviously those who will be arrested will have to be the children of the kinds of people who read this book.

The complex problems involved in drug control can be appreciated best in a consideration of amphetamines (ups) and barbiturates (downs), for these are the ones that are used most widely throughout the United States. Since they are used principally by adults and are tolerated if not actually approved by adult society, they illustrate what happens when one becomes an habitual user of any drug. Writers and truck drivers are especially prone to amphetamine addiction, and for the same reason: the drug helps the mind keep functioning when the body is fatigued. With amphetamines one can drive a truck for twenty-seven hours at a stretch or keep plugging away at the typewriter when normally he would have to quit. There is evidence that at the end of the spell the driving becomes dangerous and the typing erratic, but technically the mind is still functioning. Several times I have had an opportunity to watch the effect of amphetamines on friends and I have not envied them, for it was obvious that the benefits they gained—the drug came in many forms like Benzedrine, Dexedrine, Methedrine—were purchased at a high price in physical and nervous cost. Unquestionably they showed an increasing dependence on the drug and probably a gradual diminution of mental acuity.

What disturbed me most, however, was that after protracted use my friends became so hypertensive that they required barbiturates to relax them, and thus they lived suspended between amphetamines in the morning to pep them up for their work and barbiturates at night to make them forget it. (Barbiturates too have many names: Veronal, Luminal, Nembutal, Seconal.) It was a miserable imprisonment which not infrequently ended in an overdose of the barbiturate and near suicide, which we always referred to politely as accidental. More likely it was intentional, induced by the chaotic and unreal world into which the user had projected himself.

I hesitate to include these two drugs in the same category as marijuana because they occupy a respected place in medicine and when properly used accomplish much good. Amphetamines are helpful in controlling the latter part of the manic-depressive cycle, in dieting, and in keeping the mind alert in crisis; barbiturates tranquilize, diminish the severity and frequency of epileptic seizures, and are useful in permitting sleep when minor pain has kept the patient awake. Problems arise with abuse, which has become so widespread as to be a national concern. The ultimate comes when an habitué graduates to Dexamyl spansules, green-capped time-span-release capsules with a clever combination of an amphetamine to send you up and a barbiturate to bring you back down. Young people have a right to ask whether their use of marijuana is inherently worse than their parents' abuse of such drugs. What we should be sponsoring is a mode of life which eliminates the need for either.

3. The total percentage of homosexuals within a given society probably does not fluctuate markedly from one generation to the next, nor from one society to another; it is the relative visibility that changes according to social styles. The most savagely masculine society in which I have lived was Afghanistan, where women were kept out of sight, where men carried rifles which they used in-

stantly if insulted, and where every masculine virtue was extolled. Afghanistan had about the same percentage of male homosexuals as France, except that in the former country it was acceptable practice for male couples to walk hand in hand, embrace publicly and admit their sexual relationship. It is the most aggressively male societies—the German army, the English public school—that produce the most flagrant displays of homosexuality.

The homosexual life is a most difficult one to discharge with grace, and the fact that such lives are now more conspicuous does not mean that they are any easier. The opportunities for entering such arrangements are simpler now than they were several decades ago, but their chances for stability are no greater. For these reasons I say that the young man today faces rather more difficult problems in this area than we did.

4. The new danger young people face is alienation from society, and this risk will increase before it diminishes. Around the world I have talked with thousands of young Americans who have dropped out of the competition. With faulty logic they have persuaded themselves that no self-respecting man would subject himself to the demands of a business career, or a life in the army, or the discipline of a university or even the requirements of marriage. They equate themselves with Henry David Thoreau without being aware of the solid training from which his decisions were made or the noble purposes to which they were put. Since all artists, and especially novelists, are dropouts from their society—to a certain

degree—I have felt attracted to these young people; never have I rejected them out of hand, but the more I talked with them the more I realized that the real descendants of Thoreau are those who withdrew temporarily to study the facts and then returned with a burning desire to make things better. Among the dropouts I found a small cadre of such fellows, and they seemed among the finest young people I have ever met. If they can get their ideas straightened out, and if they can return unimpaired, they will make notable contributions to our society, and I would be very pleased if a son of mine were among them. To families whose sons have taken this course I can only say, "This is the gamble that many of the best men in history have made. I hope it works out for your boy."

As to the others, those real drifters who will never succeed in stabilizing their lives or utilizing their capacities, I am afraid they must be written off as total losses, tragic but irredeemable. There are probably more of these today than there used to be, and I see no likelihood that their number will be diminished in the decades ahead. They are the hippies, the yippies, the acidheads, the drug addicts and the totally alienated. They have always been a part of society; today they seem to be starting their downward plunge sooner.

Two facts remain. The idea seems to be gaining credence that you can lead a constructive adult life even if you do not bother to master any skill. I find no evidence to support this belief. The world will continue to be the responsibility of those who know how to do something. Competence will still be the touchstone that separates the producer from the nonproducer. For the young revolutionary who believes otherwise, a visit to nations like Russia and China would be illuminating; no other societies place a higher premium on those who have competence or a lower on those who do not. Capitalism, because it produces a surplus of consumer goods, can afford to be more patient with the incompetent. If the world of the young revolutionaries did come to pass, those who were educated, those who knew how to operate factories or manipulate money systems, would be at a treble premium. Competence is now and will always be the essential requirement for a creative life.

If I had sons who seemed to have the capacity to make a contribution, I would encourage them to take humanities courses in college, unless they demonstrated such a strong bent for medicine or engineering that they wanted to get immediately into those professions. I would recommend the study of philosophy, history, literature, the principles of science, the abstract analysis of sociology, and psychology and the theory of government. I would do so with the knowledge that in my son's senior year when the engineering firms came to college to recruit young men for high-paid jobs they would pass him by, for he would "be able to do nothing specific." But I would also know that twenty years later when our society was looking for men to run it, to head the firms, to write the persuasive books, to head the political par-

ties, they would come to him and to men trained like
him. In an age of science, the need for men trained in
humanism will be greater than ever.

Our world continues to be directed by men with
broad educations, and even the doctors and engineers
who started to specialize early will be separated in two
groups: those who continued their liberal education
after they got their degrees and those who didn't, and
the leaders of the professions will have to come from the
former group.

When I hear a pessimist growl, "I don't want to turn
this nation over to the young people I see," I wonder
what alternative he has in mind. Before the end of this
century, the young people who frighten some of us will
be running every institution in our nation. We had
therefore better work with the ones we have, for we will
have no other.

Communications

One of the reasons why life today seems more complex than it did half a century ago is the speed with which bad news communicates. A major factor in the Vietnam war has been the presence of television, which makes the actuality of war insupportable.

This raises certain interesting speculations. Abraham Lincoln would not have been able to prosecute the Civil War to a successful conclusion had television been flooding the contemporary scene with daily pictures of the northern Copperheads who opposed the war, of the draft riots that rocketed through northern cities, and especially of the stark horror of Vicksburg. Sometime in late 1863 he would have been forced to capitulate, with the probability that slavery would have continued in the southern states till the early years of this century.

Similarly, had daily television in World War I flashed back to London the horrors of the Somme and Verdun, where men strangled in mud and hung their corpses on matted barbed wire, there would have been such an outcry across England that the war would have had to end on German terms. And what would have been the effect on France if cameras had reported the history of that tragic unit which, when being led by incompetent officers into certain death, began to baa like sheep on their way to slaughter, until their officers hushed them by the simple trick of designating every tenth man and ordering him shot dead by his fellows?

The problem is that democracies insist upon free speech, and dictatorships do not, and whereas in most situations the democracies have the advantage, in some they suffer. We ought to know what these strengths and weaknesses are.

A free press is essential, and I shall not belabor this point beyond recalling a curious incident which happened some years ago in my community and which crystallized my attitude toward the press. An apparently exemplary citizen who taught Sunday school in one of our most prestigious churches was accused by a teen-age girl of indecent exposure and sexual threats. The police arrested the man but offered to keep the story out of the papers if he acknowledged his guilt and accepted a quick jail sentence. He pondered this deal for some time, then said, "I can't do it. I'm innocent and will insist upon a public trial." The police pointed out that this would mean a scarifying publicity, but he persevered.

The police were right. Local newspapers gave the story

an almost indecent exposure, featuring the Sunday-school angle, and I observed at first hand what might be termed an orgy-by-headline. In fact, the poor man was so humiliated and his family subjected to such a concentration of anguish that in the end a stranger whom no one had suspected confessed to having committed the crime, and when the accusing girl saw him she cried, "Of course! That's the one."

That is freedom of the press in a nutshell. It does not guarantee that the news will be pleasant or that the publishers will use their powers with discretion, but it does ensure that society will not fester and become corrupt, as it does in countries where there is no free press. We pay a fearfully high price for freedom, and at given intervals any one of us could tell a newspaper owner how he ought to run his paper, or a television manager what he ought to show, but we cannot devise a substitute for a free press.

Television presents special problems. We have lived with it now as a major force for about twenty years, but few appreciate how radically it will change our society in the twenty years to come. The age of television is only beginning; its true impact has not yet been felt. It will reform the world even more than the invention of printing did in 1453, for the screen is more pervasive than the book.

Education will be totally changed by television. The teaching of languages, drama and literature will be marvelously enriched; geography and history will be revolutionized; science will be taught more quickly and cheaply; one good professor will reach thousands of pupils.

We will soon start producing well-educated men and women to whom the book will be a minor aspect of culture. They will be visually oriented and will be just as alert as their book-oriented fellows, but they will learn intuitively rather than solidly. For as long as I can visualize, the solid masters of subjects will continue to learn from books, but they will be an increasingly diminished minority. Therefore I see a sharp polarization in our society between the few trained experts on the one hand and the mass of generalists, often with the most keen intelligence, on the other, and in time it will be the latter who will rule the nation.

Powerful as television will be, I doubt that it will ever deter from reading those who ought to read. I reached this conclusion about twenty years ago and gambled my adult life upon it. I reasoned, "The more popular television becomes, the more those who like to read will look for substantial books. Also, the more television they see, if it continues at the present level, the more they will appreciate long and intricate books which will engage them for several weeks. Instead of reading less they will read more." I therefore committed myself to write the kinds of books I have written, and my prediction came true. Fewer people are reading today, but those who do so read with an avidity not known before, as if each adolescent television program made the book become precious. I would expect this trend to continue, so that we may be on the verge of a period when a new Tolstoy, Dickens or Balzac could enjoy a tremendous readership, but only among a narrowing clientele.

Television is not antithetical to education. Children nurtured by the tube learn faster than others, acquire large vocabularies, build more extensive cognitive bases from which to think, and acquire horizons that are vastly expanded. Whether they have an intensive intellectual experience is open to doubt, but that they are educated is obvious. For this reason I do not fear the advent of the television generation. It will be much different from the generation reared on books, but it will not necessarily be worse and in some respects it may be better.

Television will revolutionize politics even beyond what it has to date. We have had television campaigns, but we have not yet had such a campaign directed at voters who grew up on television; that will come in 1976, and by 1980 more than half the voters will be television reared. Selection of candidates, scheduling of speeches, types of appeal for votes and methods of financing will all have to conform to what television demands. The danger of a demagoguery will be greater than before. This is a major reason why I do not want to see popular election of the President; the power of television would become overwhelming.

The possibilities of television will not be appreciated until the new system of community antennas, CATV, becomes nationwide. Then up to seventeen channels providing perfect reception will be piped into every home. Perhaps ten of the channels will offer standard programs, lifted from networks and stations up to a thousand miles away. Channel 11 could be a super-intellectual program; Channel 12, a college curriculum; Channel 13, a review of world music, played endlessly and repeated every year; Channel 14, a review of the world's best books; Channel 15, the weather, announcements of movie programs, details about community meetings; Channel 16, goverment announcements; and Channel 17, a facsimile newspaper, its pages turning endlessly throughout the day. Seventeen channels are possible right now; new cables soon to be available will bring fifty to seventy-five channels into every home. Imagine what that will mean.

In the meantime something ought to be done about television as it exists today. I am not opposed to the general programming we have; it seems to satisfy the audience, and with the addition of Ultra High Frequency stations and National Educational Television there are seven channels in my area on which even the most fastidious can usually find something worth looking at if he picks with care.

But I am amazed that our government has given these channels free of charge to private individuals and has required so little in return. I agree with Vice-President Agnew when he says that we ought, as a matter of common prudence, to review this accidental system. I do not share his apprehension that the news commentators we now see are too liberal—after all, most of them are employed by our largest and most conservative corporations, and since all of them seem to come from small towns in the South or West, I do not think of them as effete Easterners—but I do believe that television is such a persuasive force that it ought to be used more creatively. If it is going to drive magazines, motion picture theaters and many newspapers out of business, it ought to assume the tasks they used to perform and do them better.

I think it obligatory that our present system of television be taxed to support a public network which would be piped into every region in the United States and broadcast from minimum-cost relay stations so that the program would be available to almost every home. This new system would provide programming of a high quality, but not be commercially profitable for standard stations. No attempt would be made to garner a maximum audience; from the start the government would admit that there might be millions of viewers who would not be interested in what was being broadcast, but it could also be assured that those people who were concerned with the public good or their own continuing education would be watching. Two provisions would protect the interests of the commercial stations: (1) at any time during a day's broadcasting from the new system they could pick up the broadcast and send it out over their own system free of charge and with the right to add advertising if they wished; reporting on significant public events could thus be handled at less expense than by the present system, as could debates in Presidential elections; and (2) if one of the programs invented by the new system proved unusually popular, any network, upon six weeks' notice, could hire the personnel involved and thus shift the whole program over to the commercial system, providing of course that some kind of guarantee were offered to ensure that the quality of the lifted program would not be seriously diminished. At first glance such freedom to pirate from the new system might seem to doom it, but that would not be the case. There is so much talent in this nation eager to do creative work that the new system could spin off two programs a month, turn them over to commercial television without charge, and come up with two replacements that would be practically as good. The benefits from this constant infusion of new ideas would be enormous, and television would stand on the threshold of the contribution it is technically capable of making. This should be undertaken immediately, for if there is alienation among our young, much of it stems from the fact that television, one of the most extraordinary inventions of mankind, is so poorly used. If I were a young man exploding with idealism and if I saw our major networks with their banal offerings, I would question whether this were the best my society could provide. I would wonder if this represented the true values of American life, and if I concluded that it did, I would begin to doubt the validity of my society. I would be on the verge of alienation. We can do better and we must.

Of far-reaching consequence will be the continuing developments in the field of information retrieval. This will become one of the most exciting areas of specialization for young people in the forthcoming decades. Let me explain what I mean. The other day I was handed a small rectangular piece of what appeared to be celluloid. It was about the size of an airmail postage stamp and contained, on one side only, a series of minute dots printed electronically, the entire text of the Bible, Old and New Testaments alike.

Inserting this chip, as it is called, into a scanning machine, the reader can, by adjusting levers, find any chapter of the Bible he requires and project it more than full size onto a reading screen.

In a small room, chips covering every book in a city library could be filed. In a large filing case you could keep chips of every book ever published in Portugal. With relative ease you could bring into one center chips covering the entire British Museum and the Library of Congress. The possibilities are staggering. The library of the future may very well be twofold: an underground repository for precious old books published prior to 1980 which no one sees or handles, plus a crisp reading desk to which chips from any library in the world are delivered electronically as you dial for them.

Already this system, in simplified form, has produced a revolution in the exchange of advanced information. Throughout the world there are perhaps a hundred and fifty learned journals which keep scholars apprised of what is happening. They are published in all countries in editions of not more than 35,000 copies each and circulate wherever learned men are concerned about new developments. They are expensive to produce and are paid for by subscription. It could be said that the intellectual and industrial welfare of the world depends upon these journals.

But with the new copying machines which can lift a facsimile in a few moments, it is no longer necessary to print 35,000 copies of a learned journal; a corporation which used to require sixty copies of a magazine on steel processes can now subscribe to one copy and duplicate any relevant article sixty times. Consequently, these journals lose circulation at the very time when their influence increases; their revenue drops and forces them out of business when they are needed most.

This technological difficulty is simple to solve: we need only find some new way to compensate the editors. Their magazines are no longer essential, but their ideas are. I have experienced this technological problem; of the seven magazines which first published my writings, only two are still in existence. Of the five motion picture companies which made my movies, two are out of business and two others are specializing in TV films. The great newspaper for which I once went to Asia, and which then seemed so powerful, went broke because of television and ceased to publish. The paperback editions of my books are circulated by companies which were not in existence when I started to write and are sold in outlets which ten years ago had never seen a book. I would not dare to guess what writing will consist of twenty years from now. Our ideas will continue to be important, but how they will be circulated cannot be foreseen.

For some decades I have had as my hobby the building of high-fidelity systems for schools and churches, and I have recently been impressed by the possibilities of the tape cassette, a small, sealed, celluloid receptacle containing an endless circle of recording tape. Onto a cassette I transcribe any material I must learn; later I slip it into the tape player in my study or automobile and the sound comes back in perfect quality. Much of what we will want to learn as adults will be packaged in this way, to be played back at our convenience.

More exciting is the possibility, already available, of having similar cassettes which will plug into our television sets and give us precisely the visual program we want with full sound and color. These will soon be generally available to the public, prohibitively priced at first, rather cheap later on: about $8.00 to purchase an hour show, or $1.00 for a three-day rental.

Similar developments will occur in all aspects of communication. We shall be bombarded with ideas and entertainment and propaganda. Our task will be to isolate the meaningful and use it to our betterment. The extent to which we do so will determine the quality of our society.

Observers believe that the quality of life
in the United States will be determined by what steps
we take to safeguard the environment in which we live.
They point with apprehension to the rapid rate at which
we are polluting our air, contaminating our water supply, killing off our wild life and raising the noise level
of our cities. They call these processes "the uglification
of America," with special emphasis on the unplanned
manner in which our cities reach out to create ever new
urban sprawl.

I agree with these critics. Years ago I decided that
even though I was free to live anywhere in the world, I
would stick with rural Bucks County, for I had seen
nothing in my travels which surpassed it in its simple
combination of natural beauty, orderliness and nearness
to the big cities that I have enjoyed so much. I have
never regretted that choice, for life in this part of the

Philadelphia area is almost as good as it could be.

Other people might prefer other places: Princeton, New Jersey, and Santa Barbara, California, have been mentioned as nearly ideal spots in which to live, combining as they do a natural beauty with cultural richness. But the arrival of an oil slick has destroyed much of the attractiveness of the latter site. Certain villages in New England, wholly in the countryside yet close to Boston, have a similar quality, and several areas on the Main Line west of Philadelphia are better managed than the area in which I live, but on balance I picked a good spot.

What has happened? Every year of my life the land between where I live and Philadelphia has become more jumbled, more abused and uglier. And along the main highways which take me into New York the deterioration has been appalling, with forty miles of unplanned monstrosities degrading the countryside and cheapening the lives of people who live there or who pass through. Dirt, noise, ugliness, pollution and lack of care characterize this drift away from natural beauty and into a new kind of urban blight.

Let me be specific as to what I mean by this criticism and what I do not mean. I will specify the latter first.

When I was in my late teens, one of the joys of my life was traveling from Doylestown westward through Norristown to Valley Forge and down to Villanova and Swarthmore, where I was attending college. It was a journey through the best part of America, with birds and flowers and now and then a sight of deer in the distant fields. I remember with special delight how exciting it was to cross the beautiful Schuylkill River at Norristown and enter that lovely maze of roads leading to rural King of Prussia, Valley Forge and the rolling hills to the south. I never traveled this road in either direction without feeling privileged.

The other day I had occasion to make this trip again and found the area to be an undifferentiated suburb, one house or establishment after another, plus a whole new city at King of Prussia. I could have had no more dramatic introduction to the problem of conserving our natural resources than this, for the city had reached out and gobbled up one of the loveliest areas I had known.

Well, I did not object. And I do not sympathize with mere protesters who cry, "Isn't it a shame that King of Prussia has become a city?" or "Isn't it deplorable that a Levittown had to spring up in lower Bucks County?" If the area population is going to grow from 1,900,000 in 1900 to 7,500,000 in 2000, people are going to have to live somewhere and I think the creation of whole new communities is one of the sensible answers. Within the next thirty years, if our area population increases by 2,000,000, we will have to provide 500,000 new homes and they will have to go somewhere.

Changes in our patterns of local government must come if these newcomers are to find land for their houses. Our courts have begun to throw out many of the zoning ordinances used by suburban communities to keep city dwellers and other strangers out. A tight circle of exclusiveness circumscribing the city cannot be tolerated, and ordinances calling for two-acre plots or even one-acre will be declared illegal if they are too near the city and held to be operating against the general welfare. We will not then be able to ensure suburban beauty merely by maintaining large expanses of lawn; we will also have to look to the beauty of what we build on the land thus set free.

The physical look of the entire area, from the most rural edge of the New Jersey counties to the most exclusive residential areas of the Main Line, will be sharply modified. In the last five years, within a mile from my remote rural home, a dozen new houses have been built, and before long it will be a hundred. It ought to be, for homes are needed.

Therefore I do not see how one can logically object to the mushrooming of new communities or the services that tend them, which means that we shall soon be living in one unbroken urban area reaching from Washington to Boston. We cannot halt this, granted our rapid growth of population, but we can take steps to see that the growth is logical and that it preserves as much natural beauty as possible.

What I do object to is this: For the past several years my neighbors have mentioned from time to time the serious pollution of an historic stream that runs not far from my home. I listened vaguely but did nothing about it. Then Joe Livingston, the financial columnist, told me, "You've got to go down and see what's happened." So I went.

This marvelous stream in which I used to fish and where as a boy I had gone swimming, this ribbon of cool water which had been a delight to generations of farmers, was now a fetid body of yellowish water with not a living thing in it. Frogs, fish, waterlilies, bullrushes and ducks' nests had all vanished, and along the edges of the swimming hole stood shameful signs, posted by the health department:

When I inspected the stream, I found that an acid deposit perhaps an eighth of an inch thick had been cast upon the whole stream bed; this had killed every living thing, even the weeds, along the entire length of the stream to the point where it emptied into the Delaware.

What had happened? A responsible manufacturing company, which had brought much-needed jobs into our community and which we had welcomed, found it expedient to dump its chemical waste into the stream.

The local court had enjoined the company from doing this, but enforcement of the order had been impossible, so that now one of our most charming natural resources had been destroyed. (Experts assure us that if the deposit of new waste is halted, three or four years of flushing out with pure water will restore the stream. A decade of therapeutic attention might even restore Lake Erie, for nature's powers of recovery are phenomenal, as reforestation has proved.)

The loss of my stream had occurred under my nose, as it were, and with me making no protest. When I finally saw what had happened, I was ashamed of my inattention. What in those years had I been doing that was more important than saving a stream? If we continue to abuse and destroy our resources, many of us will be asking that question thirty years from now, but by then it will be too late, and some of the precious things we have lost will not be recoverable.

Shortly after publication of the preceding paragraphs, dramatic proof was given of the unexpected way a ravaged environment can strike back at the persons who have abused it. When we made public outcry against the contamination of our stream, the manufacturing company built a series of deep catchment basins into which they pumped their poisonous waste. This was not a solution to the problem, merely a postponement; the life-killing contaminants continued to seep through the bottom of the basins and into the stream in the same old way. But since the amount of flow was somewhat diminished, the visible effect was less frightening than it had been, and some of us concluded that this temporizing measure had settled the problem. The stream wouldn't be totally poisoned, only half so.

Then our area was faced with one of those ten-year cyclic accidents of a heavy snow followed immediately by a warm rain. Our valley was flooded, roads were washed out, farmers were marooned, and an unusually high crest of water threatened to overflow the manufacturing plant, flush out the catchment basins and throw 500,000 gallons of lead sulfate into our trivial little stream—and from it into the heart of the Delaware River, from which some five million people take their drinking water.

Faced by a disaster of such proportions, crews of my neighbors were summoned to pile sandbags about the catchment basins to keep the poison from overflowing. Only their strenuous efforts protected the drinking supply of a metropolitan area, and at last our whole community awakened to the monster we had allowed to grow up in our back yard. It had killed a stream. Now it could kill us.

I am not a primitivist. I do not automatically think that old ways are best, and nothing seems more inane to me than the argument that life was somehow better in colonial times because farm wives made their own soap and candles. As a boy I studied by lamplight and had to wash the lamp chimneys, and believe me, electricity is better. I am often asked if the natives in the South Pacific were not happier before the advent of canned goods and penicillin, and I counter with the question,

"Were the people happier when the life expectancy of a woman was thirty-five and a man thirty-nine?"

I am for change, and when it also represents progress I am happy. Let me explain further what I mean. One of the reasons I live where I do is that often in the morning or in the late afternoon I can see herds of deer browsing in the fields not far from where I work. I never cease to thrill at the sight of these splendid animals who share the woods with me. What have they been worth to me: untold values in relaxation and the appreciation of nature.

I am quite prepared for the fact that within a few years the pressure of population in my area will force the deer to move on. Ten years from now they will not be visible at dusk, and that will be a loss, but it will be offset by the good that the new residents in the area will enjoy from living in new homes and spacious surroundings.

Therefore I can accept the disappearance of the deer from my front lawn, but if they were to disappear altogether, as many species might if natural living areas are not preserved, I should experience a loss so great that I am not sure I would want to go on living in a world that had sacrificed so much. A good society does not require that the deer live on my lawn, but it does require that they live somewhere.

This planet, devoid of its natural inhabitants—animals and birds and fish and trees and flowers—would be a desolation. It is quite possible that men require dogs and deer to keep them human. It is possible that we need cleaner air and quieter cities to keep us sane. There is a balance between beauty and business that must not be ignored.

The quality of a good life depends in large measure on how a man reacts to his natural environment, and we cannot destroy one without diminishing the other.

Fortunately, in this area we are facing up to the problem in time. Not far from my home, four parks now operate and a fifth is about to come into being. The ravages we have permitted can be reversed. Space will be provided so that animals and birds can survive with us, and the good architecture at King of Prussia proves that the new cities which will replace the old farms can be appealing to the eye. Whether we can halt air pollution and the rapid rise in the noise level remains to be seen, but at least we have been alerted to the problem. In thirty years my hill will be completely altered. It need not be destroyed.

The Population Cancer

In the original version this book I refrained from comment on the population problem except for a statement of fact. I did so for a good reason. For some years I have served as principal fund raiser for one of the population study groups and became so constantly immersed in controversy that I deemed it unfair to inject personal concerns into what was primarily a public document. Perhaps I was unwise in this self-imposed restraint, but this is a principle which I usually follow and which I have found to be satisfactory.

But since I am now publishing this book under no sponsorship, I am not only free to state my personal convictions but am obligated to do so. My attitude is simply stated: I foresee such a rapid increase in population throughout the world that it must become like a cancer, multiplying fantastically and eating up all available sustenance to no constructive purpose. If allowed to proceed unchecked, it has got to produce catastrophe.

If the population of Latin America continues, as it has recently, to double each twenty-four years, the time must come when every cultural system operating in that area will have to be radically altered or abandoned. If India continues, as it did from 1965 to 1970, to add fourteen million new persons each year, any rational plan for the future government of the Indian subcontinent becomes meaningless. Only chaos can result.

No better example of "the futility posture"—in which a nation must run breathlessly just to stand still—need be cited than Egypt. Some years ago, with considerable diplomatic and engineering skill, Egypt constructed a high dam across the Nile, assuring the citizenry that when completed the dam would provide a regulated water supply and a new source for electrical power. Prospects for living were bright.

But in the years when the dam was being built the population of Egypt increased by such giant strides, about a million new citizens every year, that any social benefits which the dam might have yielded were discounted before the dam was finished. In the end, Egypt was worse off than when she started. And since her population is going to double every twenty-five years, she will soon be immeasurably poorer than she was before she built the dam.

The following table illustrates the problem as faced by different types of nations. The crucial column is the one entitled "Years Required to Double Population," for these index numbers best indicate what is happening.

POPULATION CHARACTERISTICS OF SIX NATIONS *

Nation	Land Area (in square miles)	Population	Density per Square Mile	Years Required to Double Population	Growth in Last Five Years
Mexico	758,259	50,700,000	67	21	8,000,000
Egypt	386,198	33,900,000	88	25	4,400,000
India	1,261,597	554,600,000	440	27	67,900,000
East Pakistan	54,501	72,300,000	1,237	21	10,900,000
Japan	142,688	103,500,000	730	63	5,500,000
United States	3,615,211	205,200,000	57	70	11,400,000
World	56,421,000	3,632,000,000	64	37	343,000,000

If each square mile of United States land were populated as heavily as India our population would be 1,580,000,000; as heavily as Japan, 2,640,000,000; as heavily as Pakistan, 4,800,000,000.

* Source: 1970 World Population Data Sheet, Population Reference Bureau. Land area from World Almanac.

"Mexico 21" should be read: "If the present rate of population growth in Mexico continues unchanged, the population will double itself in only twenty-one years."

Egypt's density index seems moderate only because so many square miles of desert are added into the computation; if only life-sustaining land were considered, her density would top the list. Indeed, as her index of 88 shows, even when the millions now huddled along the Nile valley are distributed across the desert, the concentration is still above the world level.

India's case is so appalling, with more than a million additional citizens being born each month, that certain hardheaded experts like Paul Ehrlich and the Paddock brothers, William and Paul, advise that no further outside food be sent in for humanitarian purposes. They argue that the subcontinent, including Pakistan, has become a bottomless pit in which small amounts of additional food are meaningless, since they merely encourage the production of additional people. I used to know India well and believe there is yet a chance to halt the dreadful increase. I cannot therefore agree to condemning her to internal combustion, but if her present rate of population increase continues it will not matter what outside well-wishers recommend. She will explode.

After considering problem countries like Egypt and India, one turns to his homeland and sees that it requires seventy years to double our population, twice the world average, and one is tempted to say, "We have no problem." In reality, our figure is about twice too high, since the world figure is four times too high. We too are in trouble.

What aggravates the problem is the fact that an American child will live approximately thirty years longer than an Indian child and in that time will consume natural products—food, wood, metals, fibers and furs, newsprint—ten to fifteen times more rapaciously than an Indian. Thus our 11,400,000 new citizens in the past five years are much more depleting than India's 67,900,-000. In many respects the world is better able to absorb India's increase than ours.

Americans often suppose that our increase comes because families at the lowest economic level have too many children. Wrong. The growth comes from the middle-class families whose parents are able to support their children. There are, of course, notorious cases in which a mother on relief will have a sequence of illegitimate children who then provide her with a living via the relief check, and this should be stopped, but to believe that such abuses are the cause of our population explosion is like believing that the Johnstown flood was caused by a little girl who upset her cup of tea that day.

Two difficult and tendentious points must be clarified. Blacks are wrong when they interpret public attempts at lowering the birthrate as an attack on them. And we are all wrong if we believe that the Catholic Church is to blame for our failure to grapple with this problem.

As to those black leaders who have led the fight against family planning, seeing it as a cunning move on the part of whites to limit blacks and therefore "a form of genocide," I do confess that if I were an angry young black I would so interpret the movement and would rail against it . . . for about six months. Then I would simmer down, look at the facts and ask myself some hard questions.

What nation is better off because it has a huge overpopulation? What nation has power because it has millions of extra people whom it cannot feed or house? Where is there a nation in which an overcrowded minority has gained an advantage from numbers, if its members could not live decently or gain an education? Is it the destiny of blacks to form nothing more than a growing, undigested lump at the bottom of society? And what advantage is there in having ever larger numbers of blacks if the goods and services to support them constantly diminish?

We are all in this boat together, so after my six months of railing I would awaken to the true fact that I was doing my people no service by demanding that they breed to the limit and thus condemn themselves to a life of privation. There is no black population problem as opposed to a white problem, no Asian problem as opposed to a Latin American. We are all part of the same crisis.

The results of the Papacy's unwillingness to approve mechanical methods of limiting population are usually misunderstood. People are apt to say, "Catholic countries, because of their reluctance to practice population control, produce huge human surpluses." This is not true, and people who so argue confuse the issue. The following four sets of figures illustrate the facts.

RATES OF GROWTH OF CATHOLIC AND NON-CATHOLIC NATIONS *

Catholic		Non-Catholic	
Low Rates	Yrs. Req. to Dbl. Pop.	*Low Rates*	Yrs. Req. to Dbl. Pop.
Belgium	175	East Germany	233
Ireland	100	Hungary	175
Portugal	100	Finland	175
France	88	Great Britain	140
Italy	88	Sweden	88
Spain	70	Russia	70
High Rates		*High Rates*	
Costa Rica	19	Morocco	21
Ecuador	21	Rhodesia	21
Panama	21	Syria	21
Venezuela	21	Pakistan	21
Paraguay	21	Ghana	24
Brazil	25	North Korea	25

* *Source: 1970 World Population Data Sheet*, Population Reference Bureau.

It would be difficult to find a nation more Catholic than Ireland or one in which the counsel of the priest is more significant, yet Ireland has one of the slowest rates of population growth, requiring a full century to double itself. Portugal, Spain and Italy certainly qualify as Catholic countries, yet their rate stands well below that of the rest of the world.

It is non-Catholic countries like Ghana, Syria and

Pakistan that have the runaway population growth, and in these nations the attitude of the Pope has little significance. Obviously, the population explosion here cannot be blamed on Catholic doctrine, and the generalizations yielded by this first set of comparisons is clear: it is the technologically retarded nations of Africa and Asia which produce the highest rates of growth; it is the technologically advanced nations of Europe which have the lowest, and Catholicism has nothing to do with either.

However, the second set of comparisons tells quite a different story, and here the problem has a strong Catholic characteristic. The population explosion in Latin America is of such magnitude as to constitute a world crisis. From Mexico south the numbers double every twenty-four years, and if this continues to the end of this century the Western Hemisphere will face grave problems. These nations, many of them deprived to begin with, must work at breakneck speed merely to provide their population increment with food, clothing and shelter; any chance for improvement is immediately cannibalized.

When one compares these Latin American figures with those of nations like Hungary, Finland and Great Britain, one perceives the oppressive nature of the situation. Again, the underdeveloped nations strangle themselves with people, the developed ones do not. And again this factor is more important than Catholicism.

But now the church does enter the picture, for throughout Latin America what is required is a clear-cut policy on population control, yet the church exerts such a powerful influence that such decision is not only missing but forbidden.

For me the touchstone in this area is Mexico, a nation I have known for forty years. I saw it first as a land wracked by revolution, about to declare war on the United States, and with a population of about fifteen million. I watched as it achieved pacification, a commendable amity with the United States, and a population of fifty million. What has this enormous increase produced? A group of entrepreneurs in Mexico City have grown wealthy from commissions on food and clothing sold to the millions; the peasants in the countryside are about where they were when I first saw their grandfathers. What nation is better or stronger because it has three people where one once stood? If it were possible to devise an index number for the goodness of life at a given moment and multiply it by the number of people then living, you might find that in Mexico forty years ago fifteen million people enjoyed a higher total goodness than fifty million do today. This type of value judgment will have to be made in the decades ahead by citizens of all nations, and it will be on the basis of these hard decisions that we will build our attitudes toward the population cancer.

I am not yet pessimistic about prospects for the United States, because I have lived in Japan. This country, smaller than California (142,688 square miles to 156,573) contains about six times as many people (103,-500,000 to 18,918,000) and because they practice rigid social controls they manage to live well, which leads one to conclude that if California were forced to do so, it could find a place for an additional fifty or sixty million people. If the density of population occurring in Japan operated across the United States, we would have a population thirteen times what it is now, or about 2,640,-000,000 people. But would that permit a civilization as we would want it?

The two important questions are these: Is Japan happy with her enormous population? And do we want to compete with her on this fruitless battleground? Anyone who has followed Japan's harsh struggle to limit her population knows that the answer to the first question is no, and I think it would be almost impossible to find Americans prepared to answer yes to the second.

It seems obvious that the United States could operate reasonably efficiently at double our present population; my own guess is that we could retain our democracy even if our population reached half a billion, or two and a half times what we now have.

But whether we could abide the changes that would be forced upon us is another matter. Some experts, weighing all criteria and especially the rate at which we are gobbling up our raw materials, recommend that we should start immediately to cut our population back. Pessimists sponsor a figure of about fifty million, that is, a quarter of what we have now. Others recommend one hundred million. Many believe we ought to taper off as we now are; these demographers advocate a national policy that will produce Zero Population Growth

(Z.P.G.). This can be achieved if the average family has 2.3 children, a figure which will be much discussed in the future.

I cannot make up my mind. The alternatives are too vast: from fifty million as it was at the 1880 census to half a billion as it could easily be by the middle of the next century. But I am impressed by a new line of reasoning which argues that after a certain density is reached, man himself becomes a pollutant; his environment deteriorates no matter what steps he takes to preserve it. The sewage, the garbage, the air pollution, the need for ever more highways and parking lots, the demand for larger schools and more stores, the depletion of natural resources like water and molybdenum . . . these combine to destroy the natural setting in which man thrives.

Further, if one adds the noise, the physical elbowing, the wear and distortion of the nervous system, the psychic shock of ever greater numbers of people striving through strikes and social disturbances for their share of a diminishing wealth, the frustrations of no garbage collection and trains that do not function, one is confronted by a psychological pollution that may in the end make life less worth living.

There is a real possibility that man is his own pollutant, if swarmed together in sufficient numbers, and that he does not require contaminated streams to account for his downfall. There is evidence from India and Japan to support this view, but for us to reach this dangerous level in the United States would require a population at least double what we now have. There are, however, certain experts who believe we have reached the crisis point already.

Four attractive arguments have been offered as escapes, but with them I have no patience. "Agriculture will discover new ways to feed the doubling populations." I find no evidence to support this hope. Some years ago I served as President Kennedy's chairman of a committee empowered to give away American food surpluses and learned how impossible it was to move food in large quantities to areas where it was needed, and how pitifully small our surpluses were when weighed against worldwide need. Agricultural progress can alleviate the problem but not eliminate it, for to feed adequately only the present yearly increment in Latin America would require all the agricultural effort we have plus more ships than we will ever have.

"The ocean will be farmed for radically new sources of food." This is an enticing idea, since plankton is practically pure nutriment, but anyone who has studied what has been happening in the eastern Mediterranean —where the high dam at Aswan has cut off much of the food supply that used to enter the sea through the Nile, so that fish no longer have anything to feed upon and are vanishing—knows that the ocean is a perilous farm more susceptible to extinction than we used to believe.

"If you travel across the United States you see vast empty areas that could house millions of people." I have already admitted that we could cram up to thirteen times as many people as we now have onto our land.

Obviously, if our population multiplies, the people will have to stand somewhere, but will this be called living? To establish even one new city of 200,000 in central Wyoming would require an outlay of roads, amenities, food supply systems and other infrastructures sufficient to destroy the quality of living throughout much of that area. More pertinent is the question as to whether we wish to eliminate our parks, riverbanks and open land to make our whole nation a replica of the concrete stretch from Boston to Richmond.

"Surplus population will emigrate to outer space." This alluring possibility, fed by imaginative television shows, cannot now be dismissed as easily as it might have been a decade ago, but even a quick investigation proves the futility of such hope. To build interplanetary transports capable of exporting even the million extra Egyptians born each year would eat up half the world's wealth, and constructing living quarters for them on asteroids lacking climate and oxygen would require the other half. And when the expenditure was made, we would still be faced by the 69,000,000 other newcomers added that year.

The only alternative that makes sense is to lower the birthrate. National policies should be modified to attain that end. Instead of placing premiums on large families, as leaders like Mussolini, Hitler and Stalin did, governments should discontinue help for any additional children after three, and current income-tax deductions for such children should be revoked. Public opinion should stress the desirability of smaller families and responsible parenthood. School systems should be geared to small yearly increments, and all other aspects of national planning should point toward a stabilized population. Economics has got to stop teaching that ever increasing markets are a desideratum, and businessmen must discard the old idea that the larger the population, the better chance one has of pulling down a larger share of profits. Senseless prolongation of life by contrived means must stop, and emphasis must be placed upon a good life in our productive years.

A special caution is necessary. In contemplating the population problem, citizens of the United States must take into account two factors: not only must we devise and implement a policy which will ensure an optimum society for our nation, but we must also watch carefully the runaway populations of the rest of the world so that we can adjust to the consequences that will flow therefrom. I am especially apprehensive about Mexico and the rest of Latin America, for I do not believe that we can escape involvement if their populations continue to double. Does anyone think that we could keep our southern borders closed or our food supplies intact if seven or eight million starving people started trekking toward Texas and California? If population pressures get out of hand anywhere in the world, their reverberations will be felt here.

Each of the other problems I have mentioned in this book is aggravated if our population constantly increases. Each is made more manageable if population can be stabilized. Every act of national policy must contribute to the latter, and if racial attitudes, religious customs or personal preferences have to be modified, we must modify them.

In constructing a book like this, the writer cannot escape making a fundamental choice: Shall I place major emphasis on the disasters which could overtake us if we make all the wrong choices? Or shall I stress the hopeful possibilities if we make the right ones?

Destructive forces lurk in all societies, and if we refuse to face them they will destroy us. It would be possible for the United States to collapse from any of several reasons or from a combination of them: racial tension, youthful revolution, military takeover, population cancer.

But for this to happen requires that we make one wrong decision after another and then persist in our wrong course, even when our error is pointed out to us. Is this likely to happen?

I find no evidence in American history indicating that we are so stupid. We are often tardy in our decisions and grudging in their implementation, but in our fumbling, stumbling way we do grope for right solutions and adopt them when their efficacy has been demonstrated. To deny this is to deny the pragmatic thrust of American history.

Therefore I must suppose that we will be intelligent enough to do some of the right things, and I take on faith the fact that the United States will be a functioning nation in the year 2000. It will continue to be governed, not adequately perhaps, but with its major characteristics intact. Several hundred million people will be living here, their freedoms somewhat restricted, but living nevertheless. Indeed, I can devise no alternative hypothesis, and the attractiveness of this one is that it is not only logical but provides a philosophy for continued existence.

Cynics ask, "But what if a hydrogen bomb should explode over us?" I live in the heartland of one of the world's most inviting targets, bracketed by two major cities and two major steel-producing centers. I have thought a good deal about hydrogen bombs and have soberly concluded that even if a large portion of the area I know best should be destroyed, human life of some dimension would survive elsewhere, and those who lived would necessarily operate within some kind of social structure. So the phrase "total destruction of humanity" makes no sense to me whatever. I may be destroyed; my two cities, New York and Philadelphia, may wither, and the governmental systems we have known may collapse; but humanity will continue until that day infinitely remote when the sun begins to fade or the earth is sucked into its fiery embrace.

Life will continue. The American soil will continue. It is the quality of life to be lived on that soil which is under question. If blacks and whites insist upon living in hate-filled enclaves, the quality of their living cannot be productive. If we tolerate open warfare between an established society and its revolutionary critics, the resulting life will have to be of low quality. If we encourage our population to increase without limit, we shall have to abandon many characteristics of the good life. And obviously, if we allow our educational system to collapse, we will lose many of the leaders who might have helped us attain a better quality of life.

I see no possibility that we shall erase our civilization, but I do see a real chance that we may depreciate its quality to a point at which it becomes unpalatable and scarcely worth preserving. It is against this depreciation that we fight.

What must we do to preserve a good life? I shall say no more about the seven problem areas discussed earlier, for if we are incapable of handling them, having been given the data and the potentialities, we do not deserve to survive. But there are other areas in which we must also act, and these require mention. These are the things we must do.

We must get out of Vietnam. Having lived in each of the parts of the former French Indo-China—North Vietnam, South Vietnam, Cambodia, Laos—I was originally much in favor of President Eisenhower's intention to safeguard South Vietnam's independence, and I supported President Kennedy when he pursued the policy established by his predecessor. I also wrote favorably of President Johnson's initial steps on behalf of South Vietnam's independence.

I did so because I believed that the United States ought to draw an imaginary line through various troubled parts of the world, dividing those areas in which we had no vital interest from those in which we did. I believe that this imaginary line still exists and that it delineates areas in which we cannot view with indifference the implanting of enemy forces. Cuba is such an area, and West Berlin, and Australia, and Canada and Mexico, and to argue otherwise makes no sense at all. On the day those areas collapse and fall into enemy hands, this nation is in peril; if areas like Puerto Rico, New Zealand and Ireland, to name only a few, were to be armed with enemy nuclear warheads, our continued existence would be in doubt.

I am not sure I was right when, in 1950, I concluded that South Korea was also such an area, but I participated for some years in her defense, deeming it a necessary involvement. I still think it was. The truce line finally agreed upon represented a real American victory; had Communist forces become embedded at Pusan, Japan would have been brought under severe restraint and would probably have gone Communist. The understanding worked out in Korea between communism and democracy was satisfactory to each, for it demonstrated that a balance could be attained. I hoped for a similar result in Vietnam, and if it had been attained it would have been worth the effort.

But when the buildup of American personnel in Vietnam became so much greater than seemed warranted, and when insufficient steps were taken to arrange a Korea-type line of demarcation, I became aware of the morass into which we were stumbling and began tentatively arguing for disengagement. Neither hawk nor dove, I tried to discover a course of action which would serve America's interest and concluded that our nation would be much better off if we withdrew immediately. Reasons for doing so are greater now than they were then.

The reason we should get out has little to do with Vietnam itself. Every justification for our being there in the days of Eisenhower still exists; the trouble has come at home. It stems, I think, from this. In the case of both Korea and Vietnam the United States took a gamble which no democracy can risk: we entered a full-scale war without declaring war. We neither spelled out our moral position nor enlisted public support, and every evil consequence that has followed grew out of those first wrong steps. We sought to wage war without declaring war, and this can be done only in a dictatorship.

For a democracy to prosecute a prolonged war, two conditions are essential: the conflict must have a moral justification which is apparent to everyone, and the burden of the war must be borne as equally as possible by all citizens. I know the weakness of each of these arguments. As to the first, no war can be morally justified; as to the second, the petty inconvenience of those who stay at home cannot be equated with the death and maiming of those who do the fighting. Well, men are not wholly rational; I, for example, believe that the defeat of Adolf Hitler was a necessity and was morally justified, and I would be incapable of understanding arguments of those who argued otherwise. Also, as a man at war I never kidded myself that colleagues my own age who stayed home earning good salaries were making sacrifices equal to mine, but I was satisfied that they were paying adequate taxes, that they were supporting our national commitment to the limit of their capacity, and that all of us were involved in a common effort. Only a fool expects absolute justice, but everyone has a right to expect the appearance of justice. America's unwillingness to explain the moral justification of the Korean and Vietnamese wars was deplorable; her refusal to order a mobilization that would have spread the weight of war equally on all shoulders was indefensible.

The one sure way to defeat an army is for the society which supports it to walk away from the war. This happened in Russia in 1917, in Germany in 1918, in Italy in 1944. This time it happened in the United States, and it happened because the war was being conducted immorally.

Young men were arbitrarily appointed to go out to do the dying, while others were allowed to stay at home and earn huge salaries. Businesses were permitted to make war materiel at top prices with no wartime limits on profits and no wartime taxes. There was no rationing and no disruption of ordinary life, for the government was reluctant to make the war unpalatable to those at home. A draft of the most bizarre kind was instituted and enforced by every wrong policy imaginable. And in Congress, in our newspapers, in our television shows and in our general discussion we adopted the policy of refusing to call our war a war.

Such behavior must corrode a democracy. The unfairness of picking young men arbitrarily and sending them overseas to prosecute a war which the nation as a whole rejects must sooner or later corrupt the democratic process. I first became aware of this during the Korean war and wrote a short novel focusing on the danger, but I did not make it shrill enough. We lucked our way through the Korean war apparently unscathed, but the degeneration had set in.

It developed rapidly in the Vietnam war and affected all segments of our national life. We have paid a terrible price in disaffection, debasement of our troops who engage in massacres, corruption of political channels, denigration of our universities, alienation and simple ridicule. Vietnam has become a suppurating wound which must be cauterized before it destroys the whole body.

In some respects, the worst may lie ahead. I think it remarkable that up to now the centurion complex has not manifested itself in our national life. When the Roman Empire was governed from a sensuously corrupt Rome, and stubborn legionnaires protected the holdings on distant battlefields in Germania, Dacia and Mesopotamia, there was always danger that the soldiers would get fed up with rumors of corruption at home and storm back to Rome, overthrow the degenerate government and substitute their own.

The centurion complex, as it developed among the French forces in Indo-China some years ago and subsequently in Algeria, exercised considerable influence on French politics, and there is always the danger that an American parallel might develop. Suppose that tomorrow President Truman was relieving General Mac-Arthur of his command and that the latter was stepping ashore in San Francisco at a time when students in various California universities were creating major disturbances. Can anyone doubt that there would be a cry for the General to take command and bring order into our society? We shall be lucky if we escape the centurion complex. It may already have begun to infect the blacks who served in Vietnam.

There are many reasons why the Vietnam disaster should be liquidated, but if one seeks a single excuse to make the defeat palatable it is this: the undeclared, unsupported war has had a devastating effect upon our young, and the sooner we eliminate this cause of infection the sooner we can resume one of the basic jobs of any society, the education of our youth and their introduction to society.

We must evolve a new spiritual agreement. The most profound thing that has happened during my years on earth was neither the hydrogen bomb nor man's walk on the moon; given the state of our technological advance these developments were bound to come in due time. The really terrifying thing was the degeneration of Germany, the world's best-educated nation, under the evil leadership of Adolf Hitler, for this related to man's inherent nature and threw a gloomy shadow over all men. This moral collapse proved that nations cannot survive by intelligence alone; they also require spiritual guidelines, and if these are lacking or inadequate, even the finest nation can descend to barbarism.

The United States had better beware. We have junked our old beliefs without having evolved new ones, and if we remain adrift for even one generation, we could decline into our own brand of barbarism. Democracies in particular must be careful to preserve a commonly agreed upon set of values against which to judge courses of action as they develop. Without this central core of agreement, decisions will be made on a hit-or-miss basis which always runs the risk of degenerating into opportunism or worse. Spiritually, we face this risk now.

In the past we relied upon a central agreement composed of religion, patriotic heritage, the great documents of our history, reliance upon the law, industrial morality and a belief in the equality of opportunity. It was a simplistic consensus and sometimes it didn't work, but then it was altered in response to pressures from critics who had detected the flaws. Recently it has become fashionable to describe this central core of belief and its implementing agencies as the Establishment, and it is against this that much of America has rebelled. The

problem is simple: refine it and supplant the faulty parts
with something better, a requirement which should
shock no one, since the process of refinement and sub-
stitution has been under way since the system started.
It is merely the rate of acceleration which has changed.

I say we had better beware, not because I mourn the
passing of an old and honored Establishment but because I do not see signs that we are developing a new
one. How can we do so?

Certain portions of our historic inheritance are, to use
the current phrase, non-negotiable. We are a democracy,
and if we reject the democratic process we stop being
the United States and become something else. We
operate under the covenant of the Constitution, and
whereas we may change it at will, we cannot eliminate it,
for without it we cannot hold fifty diverse states together. We are also a nation which tries to settle its
differences by law, and we had better continue to do so.
Many of the rest of our inherited conventions are nego-
tiable: public education versus private; conscripted army
versus professional; the post office as a private corporation rather than a political football; public highways
underwriting the costs of a trucking industry which
moves goods conveniently versus private ownership of
railroads which move them more economically. We can
move in many directions without losing our essential
character, provided we preserve the vital core.

But reliance upon historical precedent is not enough.
We must also agree upon certain spiritual values, and
to decide what they are and who shall define them is a

most difficult task. In trying to meet this demand we find ourselves moving into the field of religion, for to avoid ultimate moral questions when trying to determine national goals is impossible.

During my visits to various nations I have become somewhat disenchanted with organized religion, finding it as divisive as it is ameliorative. Muslim Afghanistan wars with Muslim Pakistan but cultivates friendship with Hindu India. Catholic Italy declares war whenever possible on Catholic France but leaves atheistic Yugoslavia alone. The religious bases for the enmity between Egypt and Israel and between Turkey and Greece on Cyprus are distressing, while the coming struggles in Canada, Belgium, Ireland and Sudan are especially deplorable, since here the religious divisions lie within nations and not between them.

But no matter how much one discounts the failures of religion, he must in the end come back to the moral teachers for the guidance needed. The United States at this time does not require a new church; it does require the insights which Judaism, Christianity, Islam and Buddhism have nurtured, and it is from such insights that the new spiritual agreement will evolve.

We require a new set of national goals. Where can we find them except in the inherited moral wisdom of mankind?

We must re-evaluate our national priorities. What yardsticks can we use for the job except those that spring from moral judgments?

We need a new set of values to inspire individuals.

How possibly can we devise them except from the experience of mankind?

We need new definitions in such fundamental areas as birth (abortion) and death (wholesaling of human parts such as hearts and kidneys). From what can we derive them except the teachings of philosophy and morality?

We need neither Catholic answers nor Quaker, neither Muslim nor Buddhist. We do not need answers dictated by the ritualistic preferences of one religion as opposed to another, but we do want answers derived from the inherited experience of mankind, and these are most often found in religious teachings.

If Nazi Germany had never existed and if the bestialities of the Stalin regime in Russia had not occurred, I might believe that intelligence alone could provide the guidance we need (as in the case of Germany), or that brilliant political leadership could do it (as in the case of Russia), but now I know better. A nation requires not only intelligence and political efficiency; it requires also a spiritual base upon which men can agree, and if it lacks that it is headed for trouble.

Finally, as part of this new spiritual agreement we must have a new definition of patriotism. The old one was good; it served the nation through many crises and it took me through two difficult wars, but I am embarrassed today when I observe how ineffective old forms have become in enlisting the support of our young people. In fact, insistence upon reverence for old forms could prove dangerous to our nation, for if the centurion complex of which I spoke earlier does develop it will be because soldiers living in Vietnam under the old patrio-- tism will not be able to understand, when they return home, young Americans who have rejected it and moved on to new interpretations. Twice recently I have been in motion picture houses when old-time, flag-waving movies were being shown, and the audience burst into laughter at the display of patriotic symbols which inspired me when I was a boy. A lot of symbols have lost their currency in recent years; we had better find new ones. (For example, even our time-honored definition of sovereignty will have to hold itself susceptible to review. I have long suspected that one of these days the eastern provinces of Canada will be wanting to form some kind of union with our New England states based upon a common religion and an identity of economic interests.)

Whatever form our new definition of patriotism takes, it must, as in the case of our developing a new set of national goals, be built upon the fundamental tenets upon which this nation was founded. If it were not, I would fear for our continuance.

We must distribute the benefits of our society more equitably. If our gross national product rises yearly, and if it continues to do so in the future, we must devise new ways for distributing it among our citizens. People do go hungry in the United States, they do lack the services they require for a good life, and one can, without sponsoring state socialism, recommend that radical new steps be taken in such areas as housing, food distribution, allocation of income and the utilization of trained women.

I shall confine detailed comment to one emotionally charged area which the average citizen does not normally think of as comparable to food services or housing but which does resemble them and is of even greater importance: How does an individual in this country get the health services he needs?

So much nonsense has been spoken about this subject, and it has been so completely wrapped in the cellophane of sentiment, that Americans often do not realize the truth: apart from our splendid hospitals, which are probably the best in the world, we put up with a general health service which is markedly less efficient than Russia's and not nearly so helpful when needed as England's. Partly because it was planned that way, we now suffer a lack of about 50,000 doctors. I had better be specific.

Case one. In the 1930s I received my graduate education in Scotland, whose medical schools at Glasgow, Edinburgh and Dundee were crowded with American Jews who were forbidden entrance to American medical schools. In those days, sometimes more than half the student body was composed of Americans who had sneaked into Scotland for degrees which had been denied them at home, for it was the planned policy of the American medical profession to restrict the numbers of all men seeking to be doctors, and especially Jews. I was told at the time, so often that it became drummed into me as ritual truth, that the numbers were being kept down to protect the income of those lucky few who were able to get into the American schools. In later years, as I watched those Scotland-trained doctors providing medical services for literally millions of Americans, I often wondered what would have happened to our country if these gifted Jews had not been able to gain their surreptitious degrees in Scotland.

Case two. In New Jersey I know of two hospitals serving thousands of patients which would have to close down if they could not rely on young doctors from India, Paraguay, Iran, Ghana and Pakistan. What are doctors from those nations, which need medical services so badly, doing in the United States? Why should we have to depend on them to solve our medical problems? It is sometimes argued that these young men learn their skills here and then return to serve their own people, but this explanation falls when one sees so many of the foreign doctors taking out American citizenship. We are lucky to get them. Our hospitals would have to close without them, but there is something basically immoral in a wealthy nation like ours stealing doctors from impoverished nations which need them even worse than we do.

Case three. I have recently been involved in the fortunes of a typical American family living in a rural area. Husband and wife were responsible persons who paid their bills and tried to look after themselves, but each had the misfortune to fall ill on a Friday, which in American medical practice is almost as bad as a Saturday or Sunday. The husband was hit first with what could have been a heart attack or a case of indigestion.

No doctor was immediately available, and when one was found he did not make house calls. Medication was suggested over the telephone, and the illness was treated with a heavy slug of bicarbonate of soda. The man, who was suffering from a major heart attack, nearly died; it was not until four hours later that help of any kind reached him. Fortunately, as soon as he made it to the hospital—a very good one—experts took over and he recovered. About a year later his wife, also on a Friday, was stricken with stomach pains, which were diagnosed over the telephone as intestinal influenza, then current in our area. On Saturday, Sunday and Monday her husband and I tried to get her to a doctor but succeeded only in getting more telephone advice and two new medicines. On Tuesday morning we took this woman, on our own recognizance, to the hospital, where she was operated on immediately for a ruptured appendix and advanced peritonitis. She required three operations and barely survived. In a country like Italy she would have had medical attendance within two hours and in Israel twenty minutes; in the United States it required five days, and this in one of the most favored parts of our nation.

Case four. Not far from where I live is a rural community of 2,800 which has been without a doctor for three years. The city fathers have tried every known device to lure one: free office space, outright grant for medical instruments, low-interest bank loans to cover other expenses, public sponsorship to ensure adequate income the first years. But no doctor has been available,

so that a community in one of the richest sections of
our country has been unable to purchase medical care,
regardless of how much they have been willing to pay.
When I last looked into the situation I was told, with
some excitement, that though they might be able to per-
suade a young Peruvian intern to stay in the United
States and establish his office in their town. They were
encouraged by the fact that one of the hospitals in the
next county had talked an Iraqi into staying there as
their obstetrical specialist.

We produce excellent doctors in the United States,
but not enough of them. We have the finest hospitals
in the world, but not always where they are most needed.
Our medical schools cannot be surpassed, for the few
who can squeeze into them. And as for the availability
of medical services to the average citizen, this country
ranks so far behind Russia, England and especially Israel
as to be embarrassing. The restrictive policies which
forced the brilliant young Jews of the 1930s to get their
education abroad are now bearing ugly fruit, for we
simply do not have enough doctors to serve this nation.

What can be done? We must not dilute the excel-
lence of either our medical schools or our hospitals, but
the billions of dollars that have been wasted on only
one of the casual moonshots could have been applied
under emergency conditions for the assembling of new
medical schools and the construction of new hospitals.

We should also start immediately with a training
program to produce paramedical personnel who would
handle a good share of the routine cases which now

monopolize the doctor's time. I am no longer impressed with the argument that "no case is ever routine, and each requires the attention of a full-fledged doctor." Too many nations have demonstrated that this is not a justifiable excuse for denying all patients prompt attention; inoculations, vaccinations, the setting of broken bones, preliminary questionings and the treatment of common diseases like colds can be handled by paramedical personnel trained to bring even the slightest complication to the attention of the doctor. This system works successfully in too many nations to claim that it cannot work here.

Since my experience with the unfortunate family whose members had the habit of falling sick on Friday I have come to realize that in both instances what was required was not a doctor, lured miles into the country, but some paramedical person such as I have used repeatedly in foreign countries who would say, from long experience, "This is a heart attack" or "This looks like appendicitis." Such a person could have summoned an ambulance within ten minutes, and the near-death that occurred in each instance would have been avoided.

I have belabored this one point because I wanted to show how, as a nation, we ought to be questioning all our systems of distribution. They should operate for the general welfare and not for the benefit of a few. New systems will be needed; the more ingenious we are in devising them, the better off we will all be.

We must re-establish and maintain control. I am hopeful about every aspect of American life save one.

I fear that if certain disruptive forces continue to threaten our civil peace, the average citizen will find himself so repelled that he will flee to any strong type of central government which promises control and discipline. Thus we could lose our freedom.

The disruptive forces are these: crime, gunfighting between blacks and whites, and revolutionary student activity which insults and outrages the public. By continued irresponsibility our dissidents can call into being the very thing they oppose: a dictatorship.

I have always believed that if the United States were to be thrown from its middle course it would veer to the right rather than to the left.

We are a nation whose citizens will not permit it to turn Communist, and any who dream of goading us in that direction are ignorant of our history. Before our citizens will suffer our institutions to go under, they will grab at any alternative which promises law in the land and order in the streets. I believe that if anarchy threatens, we will turn to dictatorship, with a consequent loss of freedom. I am sure this can be avoided.

Since re-establishing control is our most pressing problem, anyone who recommends it must explain his definitions. Suppression of crime does not require suspension of Constitutional rights; it does require strict laws and prompt enforcement.

Anyone devoted to our continuance as a nation will applaud the recent Supreme Court decision, fortunately unanimous, which said that if a citizen involved in a public trial behaves in such a manner as to make the conduct of that trial impossible, he can be muzzled or removed from the courtroom so that the trial can proceed. It is essential, particularly in a time of heated tempers, that public trials be conducted promptly and fairly; if the behavior of anyone makes this impossible he is striking a lethal blow against the nation, so that, while it has always been abhorrent to think of trying a man *in absentia*, if the provocation is his, the temporary suspension of his right to be in court is secondary to the right of the nation to survive. Furthermore, courts of review will look with special care at any case in which a defendant has had to be removed, to be sure that the cause was sufficient and that none of his other rights were transgressed. This laudable decision preserves both the spirit and the functioning of the Constitution.

There may be other traditional patterns of behavior which will have to be reconsidered in the light of Constitutional guarantees; the right to carry guns could be one, the right of access to dynamite another. This is not a call for abandonment of the Bill of Rights; it is recognition of the fact that a sovereign nation has an obligation to protect itself and ensure its continuity.

Ending gun battles between blacks and whites does not mean repression. I am not one who thinks that Negroes "have gone too far too fast" in seeking their civil rights. As long as there is injustice there is cause for protest, and I suspect that I will be fighting for equal rights for all Americans as long as I live, but gunfighting in the streets is not the way to gain these rights. The outrageous threats uttered by certain black leaders are neither argument nor persuasion; they are an invitation to retaliation and should be avoided. On the other hand, black groups who are trying to build a better world by Constitutional means must be reassured by our leaders that they will not be harassed.

Rebutting revolutionary protestors does not mean that protests against the draft and Vietnam need be silenced. It is possible that the citizen who protests is the patriot, for each of these adventures has brought our country much trouble. But to make the protest through vilifying our army or flaunting enemy flags or inviting assault by the police is an inflammatory game that ensures retaliation.

Finally, controlling student revolutionaries does not mean muzzling them. They have a right to question authoritarian boards or outmoded procedures, but to do so through assaults on professors or the burning of buildings is so provocative that, if persisted in, it must provoke harsh countermeasures.

What we require is a balance between protest and stability. This is never easy to obtain but is worth attempting, because we know that if through indifference we lose our liberties we shall not regain them in this century.

These are our problems: finding ways to cope with a vastly increased population, keeping youth involved in our society, reconciling race differences, protecting our environment, evolving new systems for governing metropolitan areas as cohesive units rather than as fragmented parts. To handle these problems we will need new think-ing, tough decisions and gutsy administration. Above all we must have courageous leadership, and this we deserve.

We are intelligent enough to restore control; we must do so because we are fighting for the continuance of a great democracy . . . one worth saving.